THE
JUICE
2007

The Juice
by Matt Skinner

First published in Great Britain in 2006 by Mitchell Beazley, an imprint of Octopus Publishing Group Limited, 2–4 Heron Quays, London E14 4JP.

ISBN 13: 978 184533 280 8
ISBN 10: 1 84533 280 6

A CIP catalogue record for this book is available from the British Library.

The author and publishers will be grateful for any information which will assist them in keeping future editions up-to-date. Although all reasonable care has been taken in the preparation of this book, neither the publishers nor the author can accept any liability for any consequences arising from the use thereof, or the information contained therein.

Photographs by Chris Terry

Commissioning Editor: Susanna Forbes
Concept Design: Matt Utber
Layout Design: Gaelle Lochner
Editors: Jamie Ambrose, Claudia Dowell
Production: Gary Hayes

Typeset in LubalinGraph and DIN
Printed and bound in Europe

The Juice Team and Mitchell Beazley would like to thank the following for their help in sourcing bottle images:
Alliance Wine, Anne Saussac at Perrin et Fils; Armit, Berkmann, Berry Bros. & Rudd, Bibendum, Brown Brothers UK, Chrismont, Concha y Toro UK, Constellation Wines, Dreyfus Ashby, English Wines Group, Enotria, Fairtrade, Farr Vintners, Fields Morris & Verdin, Hallgarten Wines, Jackson Nugent, John E Fells & Sons, Justerini & Brooks, Lea & Sandeman, Lay & Wheeler, Laytons, Liberty Wines, Maison Marques et Domaines, Moët Hennessy, Negociants UK, Nyetimber, OW Loeb, Pernod Ricard, Stevens Garnier, Stokes Fine Wines, Southcorp UK, Vinum, Western Wines.

Contents

The Juice 2007 – 100 wines you should be drinking

Bang! And just like that we're back. Back with another 100 wines that you should be buying, drinking, and enjoying. If this is your first time with us, welcome aboard. Each year in *The Juice*, we try to make a conscious effort to shine the spotlight on producers, big and small, who are making great wine – great wine that you can get your hands on, and more importantly, great wine that you can afford.

Over the past twelve months a lot of wine has passed our lips (tough job I know...), and what's become glaringly obvious is that the world of wine is changing really fast. A potent cocktail of modern technology, increased tourism, and fierce competition from right around the globe has meant that there's little – if any – room for sub-standard wine. The stakes (we're talking about your hard-earned cash here) are high. And while that's well and good, the flip side is an absolute ocean of mediocre wine. Not great wine, just average wine. I don't know about you, but given the choice (and money permitting), I'll take great over average any day.

I like my wine to have a bit of soul. I like to think that what I'm drinking represents a year in the life of somewhere. I like the idea that no two years will ever be exactly the same, and that much of the reason these wines are as great as they are is in no small part due to a whole load of love, blood, sweat, and tears. Naive, maybe, but I'd also like to think that I'm not alone.

Happy Drinking for 2007!

Matt

How it all works

This guide is a compilation of all the best bits from *The Juice*, a weekly email sent out to friends and workmates throughout 2006, in a vain attempt to help them drink better. To make life a bit easier for you guys, we've broken up the emails, reduced the suggestions to 100, and then re-jigged them all into one handy little survival guide.

So here's the drill. We thought that, rather than ranking the wines one to 100, it'd be far more useful if we grouped them by occasion – and so once again we've split the top 100 wines into four easy groups of 25: "Skint", "Brownie Points", "TV Dinners", and "Bling". After all, it's one of these four – love, food, too little or too much money – that usually motivates us to buy wine.

As per last year we've made every effort to ensure that both price and vintage (the current release has been reviewed wherever possible) are as accurate as possible at the time of publication, but we're only human and so are bound to make a few errors along the way.

Listed stockists are a mix of national chains, supermarkets, and smaller independent wine retailers, the idea being that you should be able to get hold of a good number of the 100 wines without too much heartache.

As ever price is key. And while we've made every attempt to track down the best bargains going around, they don't always result in cheaper wine. That said there's plenty of good options under a fiver and a stack of great wine for just a few pounds more. Finally, don't stress too much if you can't find the exact wine, ask the lovely person manning the counter of your local for a recommendation of something similar.

The rest, as they say, is up to you!

The Juice Awards

Why awards? Why not? One of the nicest parts of our job is stumbling across those "little gold nuggets" that are well worth telling the world about (that's if they don't know about them already!). Our awards are split three ways – Wine of the Year, Bargain of the Year and Producer of the Year.

And so after 12 long and (mostly) happy months slurping, spitting, and compiling tasting notes – this is the part where the wheels usually fall off – this year was no different. Rarely, if ever, are we unanimous in our chosen favourites, and as a result we end up thrashing it out until we're left with the same three wines. Worth remembering is that these are our favourite wines for the year and we make no apologies for our selection.

So without any further ado, here are the wines which in 2006 pushed our buttons for one reason, or in some cases, many!

WINE OF THE YEAR

Grosset "Polish Hill" Riesling 2005 – Clare Valley, Australia

Those of you with your fingers on the pulse will know that Riesling – be it from Austria, Germany, France or in this case, the Aussie kind – is hot. There are many, many factors that influence this award (love and money will help) but at the end of the day, the names that graced our final shortlist would all have been worth swapping your good bits for. However, this wasn't the first time that Jeffrey Grosset's wines have stopped us in our tracks – in fact year in year out these wines are rarely less than brilliant. Steely, pure, focused and dry – these are some of the most insanely well-crafted and long-lived white wines in the Southern Hemisphere.

PRODUCER OF THE YEAR

Randall Grahm – Bonny Doon Vineyards, California

The world really does need more Randall Grahms. As one of our all-time wine heroes – mainly for his refreshingly welcome (and often eccentric) take on the wine world – Grahm effortlessly knits together serious winemaking with a Monty Python-like attitude. His love affair with things European translates into a range of wines that display elegance and refinement but not at the expense of good fruit. His decision to switch his entire range from cork to screw caps for the sake of quality should also be applauded. And so it's for these and many more reasons that this year Randall Grahm earns himself The Juice Love, Blood, Sweat & Tears Award.

BARGAIN OF THE YEAR

Doña Dominga Carmenère Riserva 2004 – Colchagua, Chile

At the value end of the spectrum the competition is fierce, making this award one of the hardest to pin. Quite literally, the market is flooded with wines tailor-made to hit a price point and many of the results are ordinary to say the least. We taste plenty of them – bland, mediocre, soulless wines that at the end of the day just don't stack up. That said, every once in a while a shining light will reveal itself, in this case it just happens to be in the form of the insanely good Doña Dominga Carmenère Riserva 2004. In fact all the reds we tasted from Casa Silva were great, but this wine was in another league and punching well beyond its weight. Outstanding value.

The Varieties

Wine comes in all different shapes and sizes: big wines, little wines, fat wines, skinny wines, good wines, great wines, wines that absolutely blow your mind. And while what happens in the winery plays a big role in determining how a wine might end up, each variety has its own distinctive personality – personality you can taste!

With the number of grape varieties on the planet running into the 1000s, here's a brief run-down of the most popular – plus a few extra that popped up in this year's *Juice*.

THE WHITES

Chardonnay *(SHAR-don-ay)*

Love it or loathe it, you can't deny this grape its place in wine's hall of fame. Some of the very best examples hail from Burgundy, where texture, finesse, structure, and ageing ability rule over simple "drink-now" fruit flavours. You see, Chardonnay comes in all different shapes and sizes. Flavours range from the delicate, citrusy, and slightly honeyed styles of Chablis to the warmer, Southern Hemisphere styles, where aromas range from peaches and pears to full-throttle, ripe, tropical fruits like banana, pineapple, guava, and mango.

Chenin Blanc *(shuh-NIN blahn)*

Handier than a Swiss army knife, the globetrotting Chenin's high natural acidity and tendency to flirt with botrytis lend it equally well to a variety of styles; sweet, dry, and fizzy.

A good traveller, Chenin's stomping ground is France's Loire Valley, where it makes racy dry whites, luscious sweet wines, and clean, frothy fizz. Expect smells of green apples, gooseberries, and fresh herbs.

Gewürztraminer
(geh-VERZ-trah-MEE-ner)
Like a drag queen with too much make-up and perfume (and little shame), this is the camp member of the white-grape family. In reality, Gewürz is one of the superstar varieties of Alsace in France. The best ooze aromas of lychee, rose, orange blossom, cinnamon, ginger, and spice. Good Gewürz will be rich and weighty, with great length.

Grüner Veltliner
(GREW-ner velt-LEE-ner)
If you haven't heard of Grüner Veltliner, where have you been?! The über-cool variety of the moment, it's made in Austria and is often likened to Chardonnay for its weight and intensity, but it's spicier, with smells of miso paste, ginger, and wet wool.

Marsanne
Clean, fresh, fruity, this grape plays second fiddle to Viognier in France's northern Rhône Valley; however, it dominates many of the white-wine blends of the southern Rhône.

Expect ripe, peachy fruit flavours, fresh acidity, and barely a whiff of oak. With a bit of age, Marsanne takes on an amazing honeyed character and becomes slightly oilier, with more weight and richness. Outside France, you might see it in parts of Australia.

Muscat
For purposes of this book, the large Muscat family of grapes can be split into non-identical triplets: Muscat Blanc à Petits Grains, Muscat of Alexandria, and Muscat Ottonel. Wine styles vary from light, fizzy Moscato d'Asti (northwest Italy) and sweet, spirity Muscat de Beaumes-de-Venise (France's Rhône Valley) to Spain's aromatic Málagas and the unique liqueur Muscats of Australia's northeast Victoria.

Palomino Fino
(PAL-o-MEEN-o FEEN-o)
The most important variety in the
production of sherry, accounting for
four of the five main styles:
manzanilla, fino, amontillado, and
oloroso. Fino's the most popular and,
along with manzanilla, one of the
greatest food wines in the world. The
best are bone-dry, nutty, and
slightly salty, with awesome mineral
texture and a clean, tangy finish.

Pedro Ximénez
(PAY-dro hee-MAY-neth)
Although "PX" falls into the white-
grape family, this sun-loving
variety produces sweet, thick,
syrupy wines. Great ones are
almost black in colour, viscous,
and super-sweet, with intense
aromas of raisin and spice.

Pinot Gris/Pinot Grigio
(PEE-no gree/PEE-no GREE-jee-o)
Technically, these are the same
grape. The key difference lies in the
style. Pinot Grigio tends to be light,
delicate, and fresh, usually made
in stainless-steel tanks and best
drunk young while it's zippy and
vibrant. Pinot Gris is fatter and
richer, with more weight and
intensity, often from time spent in
oak. Pinot Grigio is commonly
found in the cool of northeast Italy,
while Pinot Gris is never more at
home than in the French region
of Alsace.

Riesling *(rees-ling)*
Technically brilliant but thought of
as pretty nerdy – Riesling currently
represents some of this planet's
great bargain wine buys. While
its spiritual home is Germany,
you'll also find world-class
examples from Austria, France,
and Australia. The best will have
beautiful, pure, citrus-fruit aromas
alongside fresh-cut flowers and
spice, with flavours of lemons,
limes, and minerals.

Sauvignon Blanc
(SO-vin-yon blahn)

Think passion-fruit, gooseberry, elderflower, blackcurrant… even cat's pee (really!). France, South Africa, Chile, and Australia all have a good crack, but New Zealand (Marlborough, to be exact) is the new home of this variety. The best examples are pale but unmistakably pungent on the nose, painfully crisp, clean, and ultra-refreshing, with plenty of zip and racy acidity.

Sémillon *(SEM-ee-yon)*

Sémillon is native to Bordeaux in France, but it's down under in New South Wales's Hunter Valley where Semillon *(no é here)* has had greatest success, producing beautifully crafted and insanely long-lived wines. In its youth, great ones explode with pear, white peach, and other ripe summer fruits. But stash a bottle away for a rainy day a few years down the line, and you'll witness its true magic: aromas of super-intense citrus fruit, even marmalade, alongside toast, honey, nuts, and sweet spice.

Verdejo *(vehr-DAY-o)*

Verdejo (not to be confused with Verdelho) is native to Spain's Rueda region, where it makes aromatic, clean, racy whites. Expect to be confused by a wave of aromatics (passion-fruit, pear, and elderflower) that will make you think you're holding a glass of New Zealand Sauvignon Blanc. The flavours are lean and citrus-tinged, with a personality not unlike Riesling.

Verdicchio *(vehr-DIK-ee-o)*

Verdicchio is grown and produced in Italy's Marches region, making big, rich whites that are pretty neutral when it comes to aroma, but super-lemony in flavour with plenty of spice and richness. Because of its weight, it can handle oak, too, so expect to see some wooded examples.

Viognier *(vee-ON-yay)*

Viognier overflows with intoxicating aromas of apricots, orange rind, and fresh-cut flowers. It's weighty, rich, and oily in flavour, with great length and beautifully soft acidity. Native to France's northern Rhône, it also shows promise in Australia and South Africa.

THE REDS

Cabernet Sauvignon *(KAB-er-nay SO-veen-yon)*

King of the red grapes, the best display power, finesse, elegance, the ability to age, and universal appeal. Its home was Bordeaux, but particularly good examples also come from Italy, Spain, Chile, Argentina, South Africa, Australia, and California. The range of flavours and aromas varies greatly, but look for blackcurrant, dark cherry, and plummy fruit alongside cedar, mint, and eucalyptus.

Carignan *(CAHR-een-yahn)*

The sun-lovin' Carignan makes full-bodied, slightly rustic, tannic reds. Once among the most widely planted red grapes on the planet, many Carignan vineyards have since been yanked out to make way for more fashionable (and reliable) Syrah and Grenache. The best come from old vines, and Languedoc-Roussillon in the south of France has some of the oldest. Carignan also pops up in the USA, Spain, and Italy.

Carmenère *(car-men-AIR)*

Carmenère can be a nightmare in the vineyard: it's hard to get ripe, and once it is, you have a tiny window in which to pick it before the acidity disappears. But when it's good, it's *really* good! Bearing an uncanny likeness to Merlot, the best are bursting with super-dark fruits (plums, blackberries, and black cherries) and aromas of spice and leather.

Grenache *(GRIN-ash)*
Grown widely in Spain, France, and Australia, Grenache is the workhorse of red grapes, and a stand-alone performer in its own right. As concentrated, weighty, fully fledged reds (especially in France's southern Rhône), the wines sit comfortably alongside some of the world's greatest. Also providing the base for many rosés: its tannin, acidity, and good whack of alcohol go perfect in pink.

Malbec
This variety loves the sun and is found in Argentina's Andes Mountains (home to a handful of the highest-altitude vineyards on earth). These are big wines, and the best are soft and super-fruity, with plums and spice.

Merlot *(MER-low)*
Merlot has long played second fiddle to Big Brother Cabernet, often sidelined for blending. Yet it's the most widely planted red grape in Bordeaux, and in recent times, both California and Australia have developed a love affair with it. New World examples tend to be plump, with ripe, plummy fruit and naturally low tannin. Wines from north of the equator are drier, leaner, and less in-your-face.

Mourvèdre *(MOOR-VED-rah)*
The star of the southern Rhône. Along with dark, sweet fruit there's mushroom, tobacco, roast lamb… even the elephant pen at the zoo! In Spain, it's known as Monastrell and Mataro, while in Australia it goes by Mataro and Mourvèdre. Because of its funkiness, it's rarely produced as a solo variety and is usually reserved for blending.

Nebbiolo *(neb-ee-O-lo)*
The best examples are layered and complex, oozing aromas of tar, roses, dark cherry, black olives, and rosemary. In great wines, concentrated fruit, firm acidity, and a wash of drying tannins ensure

they'll go the distance if you want to stash them away. Nebbiolo's home is Piedmont, where it's great with a broad range of food styles from mushrooms (truffles) to chicken, rabbit, and all sorts of game right through to old, mouldy cheeses.

Nero d'Avola (NEHR-o DAV-o-lah)

A red star of southern Italy, especially Sicily. These wines pack masses of fruit – dark plum, morello cherry – along with Mediterranean spice and earth. The best benefit from a stint in the cellar, but much is now made into well-priced wines with immediate appeal.

Pinot Noir (PEE-no nwar)

Great examples of Pinot are seductive, intriguing, even sexy; and their versatility with food is nearly unrivalled. Considered one of the lightest reds, top examples show layers of strawberry, raspberry, plum, and dark forest fruits, with aromas of earth, spice, animal, cedar, and truffle. These wines range from delicate and minerally to silky and rich. Try examples from the Côte de Nuits (Burgundy), Tasmania, and New Zealand's Central Otago and Martinborough regions.

Primitivo/Zinfandel

For ages we thought these were different varieties, but they're actually the same. Zinfandel ("Zin" for short) is found in the mighty USA, where most things big are seen as beautiful. In southern Italy, Primitivo rides high alongside Negroamaro and Nero d'Avola. With plenty of sweet, ripe fruit and aromas of violets and leather, this style is much more restrained than its transatlantic brother.

Sangiovese (SAN-gee-o-VAY-zay)

Loaded with aromas of dark cherry, plum, and forest fruits, Sangiovese often also smells of tobacco, spice, and earth. Most remember its trademark "super-drying" tannins, which, without food, can make this grape a hard slog. It's native to Tuscany, where it shines as Chianti Classico and Brunello di Montalcino. More recently, it has surfaced in Australia and the USA, but so far without the same success.

Syrah/Shiraz *(SIH-rah/SHEER-az)*
Syrah is the French name for this grape. Typically lighter in body than Shiraz, with aromas of redcurrants, raspberry, plum, and nearly always white pepper and spice. Shiraz tends to be concentrated and ripe. At its best, it oozes plum, raspberry, earth, cedar, and freshly ground pepper. Some New World winemakers are now calling their wines Syrah to reflect the difference in style from Shiraz.

Tempranillo *(tem-pra-NEE-o)*
The grand old man of Spanish wine. Native to Rioja, it has also sunk its roots in nearby Ribera del Duero, Navarra, and Priorato. Typically, it has a solid core of dark berry fruits complete with a rustic edge that relies on savoury aromas such as tobacco, spice, leather, and earth. A recent trend has been to make international styles with big colour, fruit, and oak.

Touriga Nacional *(too-REE-ga nass-ee-o-NAHL)*
Touriga plays a starring role in many of Portugal's great fortified wines as well as being an important component in more than a few of its new-wave table wines. Deep, densely fruited, leathery, and with an almost inky texture, Touriga needs time to mellow. Expect to smell things like dried fruit, leather, and violets, while fortified wines will be richer, stacked with dried-fruit flavour, and with plenty of sweetness.

The Hot
100

Skint

Brownie Points

TV Dinners

Fling

Skint

Partying, food, getting around, rent, bills, and roughly in that order – there're a million-and-one ways to spend your hard-earned cash. The reality is that, for most of us, a decent bottle of wine just isn't up the sharp end of the list. In this chapter we lift the lid on the best wines for little money. So no more excuses – what could you go without this month in order to drink better?

Casa Silva Doña Dominga Carmenère Reserva 2002
Colchagua Valley
Chile

BARGAIN OF THE YEAR

For years Carmenère has been a sore point for winemakers throughout Chile. Getting it physiologically ripe without being overripe is the real trick. Casa Silva does a brilliant job: its wines always turn out looking solid and clean. Launching straight at you with all the force of a stage dive gone awry, this is a serious attack on the senses. Deep crimson-black in colour, this wine's nose is a tightly wound mass of violet, dark chocolate and sweet, inky fruit. Delicious.

get it from…

United Kingdom
£9.99

Oddbins

Chapoutier
Belleruche Côtes du Rhône 2004
Southern Rhône
France

get it from…
United Kingdom
£6.49

Oddbins

In the wake of the heatwave that sucked pretty much every trace of regional expression from many of Europe's 2003 wines, it's nice to see local character creep back into many of the cooler and more elegant 2004s. It's cherry in colour. The nose is lifted raspberry, kirsch, smoke, and freshly ground black pepper. In the mouth, it's medium-bodied, well-fruited, and served nicely by some dark, chewy tannin.

get it from…

United Kingdom
£6.99

Olivers Wines
Robersons
Selfridges

Yalumba "Y" Series Viognier 2005 Barossa Valley Australia

Yalumba is constantly applying the spit and polish to the lower end of its portfolio, and it seems that 150 years' worth of experience has taught the company a great deal about value for money. Sourced from a mix of fruit from Barossa and Adelaide Hills, the result here is an insanely aromatic wine with truckloads of apricot/citrus fruit and exotic spice smells. The palate is inky and rich, with more ripe apricot fruit, soft acidity, and good length.

Argento
Malbec 2004
Mendoza
Argentina

get it from…
United Kingdom
£4.99

Co-op
Sainsbury's
Tesco

Once a distinguished resident of
Bordeaux, Malbec has upped roots
and found a new home – not to
mention a new lease of life – in
Argentina. With the best vineyards
tucked neatly into the foothills of
the Andes, Malbec benefits
massively from long, sunny days
and super-cool nights at altitude.
And the results? Deeply coloured,
lushly fruited, and a surprisingly
well-structured wine. Argento is
Catena's entry point and represents
insane value for money.

United Kingdom
£5.49

Majestic
Oddbins

Concha y Toro
Late-Harvest
Sauvignon Blanc 2003
Maule Valley
Chile

Laying your hands on good-value sweet wine isn't always easy, and high production costs, together with minute quantities, usually end up spoiling the fun. But thankfully it's Chilean superstar Concha y Toro to the rescue.

This is lemon yellow in colour. Bury your nose in the glass to find incredible purity of pineapple, honey, and candied citrus fruit. The palate is clean, fresh, and lively with great concentration, stunning acidity, and length. Serious "wow" factor.

Antinori
Santa Cristina IGT 2004
Tuscany
Italy

Santa Cristina, Antinori's Tuscan base, materializes in the form of a lush, fruit-driven mix of Sangiovese and Merlot. Here Merlot's job is to fill, soften, and take the edge off Sangiovese's aggressive side, while the latter provides the framework.

Packed with restrained, dark cherry/plum fruit on the nose and underpinned by smells of tobacco, earth, and spice, the palate is minerally and rich, finishing with a wash of trademark drying tannins. Great value.

get it from...

United Kingdom
£7.99

Thresher

Hardys Oomoo Shiraz 2003 McLaren Vale Australia

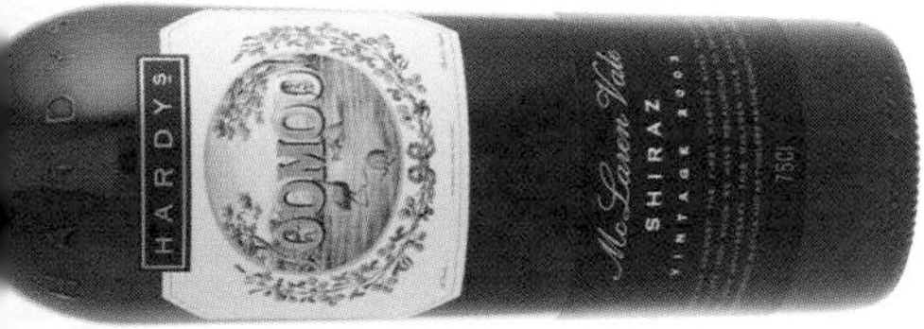

From South Oz comes Oomoo: a shoe-in qualifier for best-value red on the market. This wine provides a pure snapshot of McLaren Vale Shiraz. Here you'll find depth and concentration beyond your wildest imagination. Aromatically, plum and raspberry jam, milk chocolate, and sweet spice compete for your attention, while in your mouth, it's dense, inky, layered, and rich, with an obvious splash of good new oak. Stunning wine for the money.

Quinta de la Rosa
Val da Clara 2004
Douro
Portugal

get it from…
United Kingdom
£6.41

Oxford Wine Company

It's exciting times for Portugal. Each
year in the wine industry we get all
worked up about a country that's
going through some kind of
renaissance. Last year it was
Greece; the year before, Austria;
and this year it seems to be
Portugal's turn. Known principally
for the quality of its fortified wines, it's
Portugal's new wave of dry red
table wines that is currently creating
all the hype. Sweet plum, semi-dried
fruit, spice, and cedar dominate the
nose here, while in the mouth it is
firm, chunky, and rich.

Peter Lehmann
Barossa Semillon 2004
Barossa Valley
Australia

get it from...

United Kingdom
£4.99

Oddbins
Sainsbury's
Tesco

The team at Peter Lehmann delivers some incredible wines considering what they end up charging for them. Great Semillon produces beautifully crafted and insanely long-lived examples which, like this, appear yellowish-green in colour, while the nose explodes with lifted lemon zest and green-apple fruit. In the mouth, it's ripe and citrusy, with a tight, zippy finish.

To witness the real magic of this variety, buy an armful of bottles, drink one now, and save the rest for a few years down the track.

Plantagenet Hazard Hill
Shiraz 2004
Great Southern
Australia

get it from...
United Kingdom
£8.95

unwined.co.uk

Hailing from Western Australia,
Hazard Hill is a well-polished
example of cool-climate Shiraz,
and right on the money: chock-full
of dark cherry, plum, and forest
berry fruit with supporting aromas
of pepper, tobacco leaf, and five
spice. The palate is rich and long
and would make an ideal partner
for all kinds of meat-oriented
stuff – particularly that hailing
from the BBQ!

Seeking Closure
Friday, 19 August 2005, 12:52pm

You will probably notice that a decent chunk of the wines featured in this year's guide come sporting a screwcap.

First, screwcaps aren't bad, and second, they don't mean cheap. On the contrary, fractionally more expensive than corks, both screwcaps and glass tops (Austria's brilliant contribution to the alternative closure market) exist for one very good reason.

At the time of two-finger typing these words, it's estimated that somewhere in the range of 5 to 7 per cent of all wine bottled under a conventional cork ends up contaminated – to some degree – by a compound known as 2,4,6-trichloranisole, or TCA for short. Now while TCA isn't harmful for you to drink, it's not all that enjoyable to smell or taste, and at worst will strip your wine of all its lovely aroma and flavour, leaving behind a smell of damp, musty cardboard. Not nice.

And while sinking a corkscrew into either screwcaps and glass tops might prove both difficult and dangerous, what they do – as unromantic as they may be – is guarantee that 99.9 per cent of the time the contents of the bottle will taste as the winemaker intended. Surely that's a good thing? We think so.

Don't get me wrong: I love corks. In fact, all my best wine experiences have involved wines that were sealed with a conventional cork. But so, too, were my worst.

get it from…

United Kingdom
£9.50

Booths
Luvians
Magnums

Springfield Estate
Life from Stone
Sauvignon Blanc 2005
Robertson
South Africa

Pale to the point of verging on the anaemic, this wine lies in waiting for you to stick your nose into the glass and once you do…WHACK! It hits you smack between the eyes with a barrage of nervy Sauvignon purity and deranged freshness. Gooseberry and cassis dominate alongside smells of cut grass and freshly shelled peas. The palate is like a samurai showdown, with focused fruit intensity and razor-sharp acidity.

Torres
Viña Sol 2005
Penedès
Spain

get it from…
United Kingdom
£4.99

Morrisons
Sainsbury's

It would seem that Viña Sol is verging on becoming an international treasure. People love it – and love to tell you how much they love it. Words like "safe", "value", and "consistency" usually follow in the same sentence. Catalan variety Parellada, also used in Cava production, is the star here displaying white peach, pear, and apple fruit. In your mouth, it's soft, light, and round, with ripe stone fruit, no oak, and a clean, dry finish.

Brown Brothers
Moscato 2005
King Valley
Australia

get it from…

United Kingdom
£4.99

Tesco

Breakfast wine – another concept that got me into trouble… Still, I love Moscato with a vengeance. Think fresh grape juice, add a healthy dose of really small bubbles, and there you have it: Moscato. Simple as that. Brown Brothers regularly reference the region's strong Italian heritage with a range of well-judged Italian varietals, Moscato being one. And with a price tag that mirrors the 5 per cent alcohol, you could – if you wanted – drink this wine for lunch, dinner, and yes, breakfast too if you want!

get it from…

United Kingdom
£6.99

Adnams Wine

Hugel et Fils
Gentil "Hugel" 2004
Alsace
France

Five of the planet's most uncool grape varieties (although Riesling is a heartbeat away from being so cool it's scary) come together *Ocean's 11*-style to seduce you blatantly, then steal your heart. An aromatic cocktail of Sylvaner, Pinot Gris, Muscat, Riesling, and Gewürztraminer, Gentil is heavy on smells of jasmine, rose, musk, and orange, while in your mouth it shows great weight and spice.

Available in the UK as Les Fleurs d'Alsace, this is a consistently brilliant and affordable wine from one of Alsace's finest producers.

Jacob's Creek
Shiraz Rosé 2005
Barossa Valley
Australia

get it from…
United Kingdom
£5.68

Tesco

It's well and truly time to leave any preconceived ideas of what rosé is (or who you think drinks it) at the front door. Rosé is back – well, at least in my world it is anyway! Salmon pink in colour, the nose of this wine has lifted strawberry/raspberry fruit with just a touch of citrus. In the mouth, it's clean, fresh, fruity, and direct, with good length of flavour and a dry, snappy finish.

Boekenhoutskloof
The Wolftrap 2005
Western Cape
South Africa

From the stables of Boekenhoutskloof
and Porcupine Ridge comes the
mega-value Wolftrap red. A
medium-bodied, nicely fruited, rustic
blend of several grape varieties, The
Wolftrap is well worth seeking out.
To be exact, the blend consists of
65 per cent Syrah, 19 per cent
Cinsault, 11 per cent Mourvèdre
and 5 per cent Viognier. Got it?
Good. Nice spicy fruit on the nose
together with a savoury edge all
add to the appeal.

Cono Sur
Pinot Noir 2005
Rapel Valley
Chile

get it from...

United Kingdom
£5.49

Majestic
Somerfield
Waitrose

Not a play on words, but rather
a nickname for the cone-shaped
tip of South America, Cono Sur
produces a dizzying range of wines
from a number of regions up and
down Chile. Burgundy it's not, but
this is unbelievably good Pinot Noir
for a ridiculously small amount of
money. Sweet cherry and mild spice
character rule the nose, while the
palate, too, is unmistakably Pinot
Noir, with clean, fresh fruit, superfine tannin, and good length.

Evans & Tate
Sauvignon Blanc/Semillon 2004
Margaret River
Australia

get it from…

United Kingdom
£9.99

JT Davis
Rodney Densem
Philglas & Swiggot

If you've developed a taste for New Zealand Sauvignon Blanc in recent times but are struggling to fund your habit – or just looking for an addition to the repertoire – take a look at this snappy-priced Sauv/Sem blend from Western Australia. Pale, almost water-like to look at, on the nose there's a stack of punchy gooseberry and restrained tropical fruit, while the palate is lean, tight, and racy, with a mineral texture and razor-sharp acidity.

Seppelt
Original Sparkling Shiraz 2002
Multi-regional blend
Australia

get it from…
United Kingdom
£9.99

Oddbins

It may not be the most sophisticated wine on the planet, but decent sparkling red is the great social lubricant and a sure-fire way to get any party swinging! Seppelt is the king of this genre, and one big sniff will reveal masses of dark plum, sweet-and-sour cherry, and a touch of soy and five spice. In the mouth it's sweet, rich, just a little bit tannic, and clean – and all at the same time. Wow!

Ermita Veracruz
Verdejo 2005
Rueda
Spain

One of the most exciting parts of our drinking year has been the amount of great wine we've tasted from Spain, particularly "good-value" whites from Rueda. Made from 100 per cent Verdejo, the wine appears pale lemon in colour with green tinges. Take a sniff and try convincing yourself that you haven't just opened a bottle of Kiwi Sauvignon Blanc by accident. The flavour's more Riesling-like, with a core of rich, limey fruit, great focus, and balanced acidity.

Drinking Problem
Friday, 2 October 2005, 1:33pm

I drink alone. Well, not technically "alone", but with Carls being pregnant and off the booze, recent dinners, both out and at home, have witnessed me hitting the bottle solo. If I were clever, drinking by the glass would probably be the best (and most economical) way to go. Sadly, one too many bad experiences with "wines by the glass" – wines that tasted as though they may have been opened sometime last century – usually sees me choosing a bottle from the list.

So what's the problem, then? Well, as pathetic as it sounds, the problem for me is simply finishing a bottle without being totally wrecked (much to Carls' amusement) – not that it says anywhere that I have to drink it all in one go...

Anyway, leftover wine is a tricky one and how long it will keep once you've cracked it open will all depend on what it is, where it's from, and how much liquid is left in the bottle. As a rule, lighter whites will oxidize faster than full-bodied reds, but no matter what type or style you're talking about, wine is a living, breathing thing and, once opened, its lifespan is rapidly accelerated (think Mel Gibson in *Forever Young*). Leave it in contact with oxygen long enough and it will become vinegar.

I've had a go at all the gadgets, too: rubber seals, vacuum pumps, nitrogen (even Mum's tin foil and rubber-band method). And you know what? They all do much the same thing as simply shoving a cork back in the top of the bottle.

I kid you not.

Jacob's Creek
Reserve Riesling 2003
Multi-regional blend
Australia

It shouldn't really come as a surprise that amazingly good (and good-value) Riesling can be produced by one of the biggest wine brands on the planet (Steingarten Riesling, one of Oz's finest, is a fellow stablemate). But the bad news is that its popularity is finally on the up, and so, too, are Riesling prices in general. Bearing all the hallmarks of great Riesling – citrus fruit, mineral, spice, and steely-like structure – this wine is a massive winner. Discover it before it's too late!

get it from...
United Kingdom
£5.99

Liberty Wines

Colonia Las Liebres
Bonarda 2003
Mendoza
Argentina

Complete with a Fred Flintstone flashback of a label, this wine is supercharged on all fronts. And for your trouble you'll get big colour, a mouthful of rich, inky fruit, and some dry, chewy fruit tannin just for good measure. Along with the ridiculously low price, the fact that flying winemaker Alberto Antonini (a man who must be racking up some serious frequent-flyer points at present) has had a hand in its creation is all the more reason to go and load your boot with it.

Michel Laroche
Chablis 2004
Burgundy
France

Michel Laroche is a brave man.
To be the first high-profile French
producer to release commercial
quantities of his wines – some at
premier and *grand cru* quality –
under screwcap takes serious
guts. God only knows what his
neighbours must think, but we think
it's great and the wines are all the
better for it. This example is clean,
citrusy, and ever so slightly honeyed
on the nose. The palate is delicate
and mineral-tipped, with great
length and balance. Bravo.
Vive la révolution!

Case in Hand
Friday, 5 May 2005, 11:33am

With most of you having now (wisely) all but ditched those crazy New Year's detox programmes, a sense of spring in the air, and a four-day weekend hanging around the end of this month like flies around Josh Frost, it's time to get organized and hop into your local wine shop/supermarket and stock up for the May bank-holiday break.

For most of us, four days off means more than just "a few bottles", with reality suggesting something more along the lines of double figures. So in saying that, why not consider buying a mixed dozen? Relax: you won't be branded an alcoholic (well, not by me, anyway), nor do you have to drink it all at once. In fact, in most cases buying like this can further reduce the price of your wine, with some retailers offering as much as 15 per cent discount on straight or mixed dozens.

Having said that, the best thing about buying an armful of bottles means that you get to try a whole stack of new and different things. So what are you waiting for? Go get chummy with those people manning the counter of your local wine shop – they just might end up being some of the best friends you've ever made!

Penfolds Rawson's Retreat Chardonnay 2004
Multi-regional blend
Australia

get it from…

United Kingdom
£5.99

Tesco

For some of us, just the very thought of drinking big-company Chardonnay is about as exciting as the prospect of having teeth pulled… But this is different, and the fact that it's been overseen by Penfolds wine supremo Peter Gago makes it a far from painful proposition.

Ripe peach and nectarine fruit dominate the nose here, while in the mouth you're in for a sun-soaked hit of tropical love. There's nice balance, too, with fresh acidity and good length being the keys to success.

Montana Reserve
Barrique Matured Pinot Noir 2004
Marlborough
New Zealand

get it from…

United Kingdom
£10.49

Oddbins

Montana has forged a reputation as a producer of great-value wines that display brilliant varietal definition. Time and time again we've stated just how hard it is to tailor decent Pinot Noir to a budget, but fortunately for you, Montana is amazingly good at it. Richly fruited, there's cherry and raspberry confit alongside smells of cinnamon, nutmeg, and cedar. The palate is soft and round, and displays terrific purity and balance. Brilliant value for money.

Love Juice
Friday, 10 February 2006, 2:23pm

Far from an appropriate title, I know, but you have to admit it's very fitting for this week's piece with Valentine's Day on top of us. Sorry.

So with that out of the way and just in case you'd forgotten (!), 14 February is the international day of romance: a day when declarations of undying love – some of them completely off the wall – are made far and wide. And if you're stuck for ideas on what to get your better half, toy boy, pimp daddy, *shnann*, ho, missus, bird, bloke, shag, ball and chain, bee-arch, handbrake, trouble-and-strife (thanks, everyone in the office, for that!), how about something really original – like, say, wine or chocolate? Just don't give them together.

Chocolate and wine: two things that get most of us more than just a little bit excited. Both are aphrodisiacs in their own right, yet it's strange that, together, they should share such a rocky relationship. A combination of chocolate's tricky textures, extreme sweetness – or, at the other end of the spectrum, extreme bitterness – eliminates all but a handful of wines from the list of potential perfect matches.

From experience, Muscat-based sweet wines provide some of the most successful matches, although weird and wonderful things like sparkling Shiraz from Australia, Recioto della Valpolicella from Italy, and Pedro Ximénez from Spain all have the potential to blow minds if paired up with the right chocolate dishes.

Happy swooning!

Brownie Points

You've got a new girlfriend; maybe a pay rise from the boss is on the cards. Perhaps you're meeting the "in-laws to be" for the very first time, or you're off to dinner with friends who know a thing or two about wine. You forgot your dad's birthday; you need to make an apology, a bribe. Perhaps it's for love, maybe it's for money, it might even be for both. Whatever the reason, the following 25 wines are for those times when first impressions mean *everything*.

Innocent Bystander
Shiraz/Viognier 2004
Yarra Valley
Australia

get it from…
United Kingdom
£10.99

Cellarmarque
Define Food and Wine
Luvians Bottle Shop

Giant Steps (1960), the first full-length John Coltrane album made up of entirely original material, is genius. It also happens to be the name of Phil and Allison Sexton's Yarra Valley property, and home to wines under the Sexton, Giant Steps, and recently added Innocent Bystander labels. Neon-cherry to look at, this wine has a nose that almost jumps on you, with scents of ripe raspberry, pepper, dried apricot, and spice. Viognier adds weight to a mouthful of wine that is soft, dry, and perfectly balanced.

Alain Graillot
Crozes-Hermitage 2004
Northern Rhône
France

Since the mid-eighties, Alain Graillot has been carving out some of the purest expressions of Syrah anywhere. The heatwave of 2003 has delivered a wine with more richness than you'd normally expect to find in Graillot's wines. Gone is the trademark Crozes pepper and spice, and in its place ripe plum/blackberry fruit is coupled with rustic spice. The palate is restrained and minerally, with sweet, plummy fruit and gentle, drying tannins.

Yarra Yarra
Cabernet 1999
Yarra Valley
Australia

get it from…
United Kingdom
£12.25

John Armit Wines

An uncanny ability to effortlessly
juggle elegance and finesse with
depth and concentration – even in
the toughest of years – has won Ian
Maclean a devoted following of fans
right around the globe. This wine is
a sum of many parts, not just fruit.
It's all here: earth, undergrowth,
cedar, smoke, and spice wrapped
around a solid core of dark plum
and cassis-like fruit, while the palate
is rich, structured, and long. In a
word, beautiful.

Head-wetters
Friday, 27 January 2006, 1:17pm

Right in the middle of becoming an armchair expert on all things from bassinettes to breast pumps, I was struck by one major oversight: what were we going to drink when Junior Skinner was born? And so the hunt was on.

Champagne seemed like an obvious choice. But with an ocean of growers in Champagne whose quality can be as varied as the number of producers is great, what would I choose? Champagne, after all, is a region in northeast France where, thanks to some ancient chalky soils, a marginal climate, and a few spectacular mistakes, we now have the world's foremost celebratory drink and wine's most significant contribution to the luxury-goods industry. Producer aside, most Champagne houses make a number of different wines. Non-vintage Champagne is the most common and sets the tone for a house style. It's a jigsaw puzzle assembled from wines from multiple years and is intended to remain consistent year in, year out. Vintage Champagne, on the other hand, is produced only in particular years where the producer believes Mother Nature has been truly kind, the aim being to provide a crystal-clear snapshot of that year.

And so, on 10 January 2006, Indi Mae Skinner rocketed into the world – safe, sound, and early enough that I still hadn't managed to lay my hands on "The Bottle". That first celebratory drink came along a few days later, not in the shape of the vintage Champagne I'd hoped for, but rather as a pint of Adnams Broadside with my best mate CT. Could have been a whole lot worse, I guess?

get it from…

United Kingdom
£46

Vinum

Donnafugata
Mille e una Notte 2002
Sicily
Italy

Dotted in stars and rich in promise – this is "Thousand and one Nights", or "*Mille e una Notte*", depicted on the label of Sicilian superstar Donnafugata's "slick as you like" flagship red. Little short of pure magic, this is a gentle giant of a wine with masses of densely planted low yielding inky-dark Nero d'Avola fruit counter-balanced by delicate mineral intensity, beautifully used wood, and fine drying tannin. *Perfecto*!

Charles Melton
Rose of Virginia 2006
Barossa Valley
Australia

It's fair to say that the 2006 edition of *The Juice* was a bit of a rosé fest. However, one notable omission from last year's guide was Charles Melton's Rose of Virginia from South Oz's Barossa Valley. Yes, the extremely talented and mustachioed one is back with his second entry – this time in the form of a full-bodied, bone-dry, clean-as-a-whistle, spankingly fresh rosé. Assembled mainly from Grenache for colour and structure, this should be – if it's not already – your new favourite drink of summer. It's ours!

Kumeu River
Chardonnay 2004
Auckland
New Zealand

Michael Brajkovich is the "master" when it comes to creating complex, nutty, citrus-laden examples of Chardonnay that ooze personality and style.

From tightly packed and intense grapefruit character through to smells of cashew and hazelnut, this is a lesson in just how good New World Chardonnay can be. Better still, it tastes every inch as good as it smells, with focused citrus fruit, great length of flavour, and screwcapped freshness.

get it from…

United Kingdom
£15.00

Harvey Nichols
Vinoteca
Wimbledon Wine Cellars

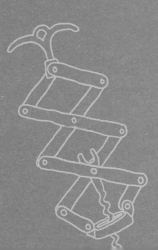

Raise Your Glass
Friday, 17 February 2006, 2:01pm

Let's face it: it's not the easiest of situations in which to find yourself. In fact, for most of us, having to choose and order wine in a restaurant represents the kind of nightmare that manages to be both intimidating and uncomfortable at the same time – kind of like the changing rooms at my gym…

Anyhow, there you are. If you're really unlucky, it might even be date number one – food order's in, you're quietly enjoying one another's company and *POP!* The bubble bursts. From above (in the poshest tone possible) comes a booming voice: "Would you care to choose some wine from our extensive, award-winning, highly acclaimed, literary masterpiece of a wine list?" Your voice breaks like you're 12 again, and you nearly wet yourself in fear. "No, thank you," you squeak.

No, thank you. What? It's time to take the power back. Next time you find yourself in the same position, remember the following points.

Make use of the sommelier – that's what we're there for. Never forget that it's your money and you have the right to drink well. The more information you can give us – grape, country, budget – the greater the chance we're going to find you something you'll love. Next, when the wine's presented at the table, check that it's the right wine/vintage/producer, then when the sommelier pours a splash into your glass, give it a swirl, have a smell, and so long as it doesn't smell like wet cardboard or dry sherry (unless of course that's what you ordered), acknowledge it and away we go. If you're in doubt, get the sommelier to check it for you. Finally, *relax*. It's only wine!

Grosset
Polish Hill Riesling 2005
Clare Valley
Australia

get it from…

United Kingdom
£14.99

Philglas & Swiggot

WINE OF THE YEAR

Riesling-lovers will understand (and probably share) my enthusiasm for Jeffrey Grosset's wines. Arguably one of the most talented Riesling producers in the world, Grosset's single-vineyard Rieslings, Polish Hill and Watervale, are easily the finest south of the equator. Complete with a screwcap (yes, we all know how good they are), this wine is simply an essay in purity. From the moment you bury your nose in the glass, it's super lime, spice, and mineral intensity all the way. Will definitely benefit from a few years left alone.

Clos de los Siete 2004
Mendoza
Argentina

The Midas touch of Michel Rolland is here for all to taste in the brilliant and super-affordable Clos de los Siete. Situated in the Tunuyan commune, south of Mendoza, Argentina, Rolland and Co have spared no expense here. Constructed from a blend of Malbec, Merlot, Cabernet Sauvignon and Syrah, Clos de los Siete is inky black to look at, with smells of dark fruits, leather, and cherry oak. The palate is lush, lush, lush with masses of fruit, and a balanced, dry, grippy finish. Brilliant.

Yarra Burn
Pinot Noir/Chardonnay/
Pinot Meunier 2001
Yarra Valley
Australia

get it from…

United Kingdom
£12.99

Bedales
Revelstoke
Savage Selection
Soho Wines

Ed Carr is the Jedi master of Australian sparkling-wine production. As chief sparkling winemaker for BRL Hardy (owner of Yarra Burn), Carr is required to produce and oversee the production of numerous labels, from Sir James right the way through to the flagship (and pricey) Arras. Carr's finger is right on the pulse here with a wine that totally over-delivers for the money. Rich and toasty on the nose, the palate, too, is rich, with intense citrus fruit, great length of flavour, and a fine, persistent bead.

get it from…

United Kingdom
£11.95

Cooden Cellars

Dr. Unger
Alte Reben Ried Oberfeld
Grüner Veltliner 2004
Kremstal
Austria

While Austria's "most famous" grape is sweeping the international wine trade off its feet, the truth is that it has yet to make a dent in the hearts and minds of wine-loving consumers far and wide. So what's all the fuss about, then? Prepare yourself for ripe stone fruits coupled with smells of wet wool, pepper, and spice. In the mouth, GV is typically steely and rich, with fresh acidity that lends this variety brilliantly to a range of ingredients and food styles. Discover it now.

Lord of the Rings
Friday, 21 October 2005, 12:17pm

Yep, that's right. The games of the XXVIII Olympiad officially took place in Athens a few years back, and for the better part of two weeks, sports fans around the planet gorged themselves on a dizzying range of quality games such as handball, shuttlecock, Greco-Roman wrestling, rhythmic gymnastics, synchronized swimming… even underwater hockey!

But the fact that the games returned to their rightful birthplace is kind of bizarre. You see not only did the Greeks invent the Olympics, but 6000 years earlier there is some pretty damning evidence to suggest that they invented wine, too. Nice work! But wait – it gets better… The ironic part is that even though the road to the present has been more than just a little rocky, right now the Greek wine scene – just like the whole Greek Olympic production – has never looked in better shape.

Screwcaps, posh new wineries, great international press – even the first Greek Master of Wine – have all been the result of a deliberate 20-year Herculean push to haul Greece's wine industry into modern times. You'll find all the usual suspects here, too: Cabernet Sauvignon, Syrah, Chardonnay, and Viognier are right at home alongside less familiar local varieties such as Assyrtiko, Malagousia, and Agiorgitiko. And with a rash of suitable growing areas dotted around the country, a combination of low rainfall, little irrigation, and plenty of volcanic ash has ensured that, right now, the very best of Greece's offerings (mainly in the form of dry, summery whites) are coming off the picture-perfect island of Santorini. Catch them while you can.

Cosme Palacio y Hermanos
Rioja 2002
Rioja
Spain

It's nice to taste Rioja that doesn't automatically have you conjuring up images of Arnold Schwarzenegger as Mr Universe. This is straight-up, good, old-fashioned Rioja: no muscle and nothing artificial – well, at least it tastes that way.

Almost brick in colour to look at, the nose is dark cherry and dried fruits together with fresh-rolled tobacco and sweet spice. It falls toward the lighter side of medium-bodied and provides brilliant value for money.

Joseph Drouhin
Chablis 2004
Burgundy
France

Made from 100 per cent
Chardonnay and with zero oak
influence, Joseph Drouhin Chablis
2004 provides a brilliant "drink me
now" opportunity. Displaying the
hallmarks of a great Chablis, the
nose has amplified notes of
honeysuckle, pear, river rock, and
cashew while the palate is rich with
soft stone fruit and minerals leading
the charge. An ideal partner to
freshly shucked oysters, lighter
seafood dishes or simply to stash in
the cellar for the summer coming.

Donny Goodmac
Shiraz 2004
Heathcote
Australia

get it from…
United Kingdom
£12.25

John Armit Wines

Believe the hype. Few wines can
boast such a cult-like following of
fans that includes everyone from
wine writers to strippers.

The ups? "The Pig" (as it's known
affectionately due to the porker on
the label) is top-drawer Heathcote
Shiraz that receives a serious dose of
TLC in the winery from one very
talented Kate Goodman. And the
downs? Limited production aside,
the owner's remaining primary focus
is greyhounds – yes, greyhounds –
and that should be a lesson to us all.
Oink.

Masi Tupungato
Passo Doble 2004
Mendoza
Argentina

get it from…

United Kingdom
£8.99

Imbibros
Mill Hill Wines
Selfridges

If your job appraisal's just around the corner and the boss fancies his/her reds packing a few extra pounds, stop here. Applying a double-fermentation technique that sees new wine re-fermented over whole, semi-dried grapes, Masi pairs up Argentina's finest grape (Malbec) with the superstar of the Veneto (Corvina).

Dense, chewy, and rich, with scents and flavours of sweet, dark plum/cherry fruit, liquorice, bitter chocolate, and Christmas cake – this should be enough to secure that salary increase you've been holding out for!

Pol Roger
Brut NV
Champagne
France

Perhaps the most under-appreciated non-vintage fizz on the market, Pol Roger is simply an essay in style and value. Bone-dry, and beautifully crafted, this wine really comes into its own as the perfect pre-lunch/dinner apéritif. Incredible aromas and flavours of fresh bread, marzipan, and citrus marmalade. In the mouth, it's lean, tight, and bone-dry – the perfect recipe to get your appetite going. If you see it, buy it!

Don't Believe the Hype
Friday, 9 December 2005, 1:33pm

Over the past two decades, Australia's big reds – particularly those from south Oz – have developed a swelling legion of fans around the planet. But it hasn't all been smooth sailing. Increased popularity has, to some degree, come at a price, and in the case of big Aussie reds, it's the local consumer who's footing the bill.

A handful of big scores and a lavish amount of praise from a handful of international wine critics have seen the overnight elevation of once dependable household names into serious "rock-star" territory. The result (which is even more worrying) is the trend toward creating wines – some tipping the scales at a whopping 17 per cent alcohol – that are so densely coloured, so massively fruited, so ridiculously woody, and so obviously formulated for points that they border on being undrinkable. And that's if you and I can afford them in the first place.

Don't get me wrong. There's nothing the matter with big – just so long as you have balance, too. Balance is the key ingredient to the success of not only our, but any great wine. At a recent London tasting of just over 200 of Australia's finest Shiraz wines, it was so satisfying (and such a relief) to see that the wines which scored well were examples that displayed a nicely woven mix of regional character, power, elegance, and silky winemaking. Better news for you was finding out that most of these same wines were still well and truly within our budgets!

Bay of Fires Tigress
Pinot Noir 2003
Tamar Valley
Tasmania

Over time the Yarra Valley,
Gippsland, and the Mornington
and Bellarine Peninsulas have set
the pace for Australian Pinot, but
a recent rise in the number of
staggeringly good wines from
Tasmania has really thrown a cat
among the pigeons. And, while
Tassie might not have vine age on
its side, its unique microclimate
makes it perfectly suited to
producing great Pinot Noir – BRL
Hardy's Bay of Fires' Tigress label is
a beacon among the island's more
affordable options.

Casa Lapostolle
Cuvée Alexandre Merlot 2004
Colchagua Valley
Chile

get it from…

United Kingdom
£13.99

Booths Supermarkets
Harrods
The Wine Society

Trail-blazing for the better part of the last decade, Casa Lapostolle knits Alexandra Marnier-Lapostolle's vision (and newly blinged-out winery) together with top consultant oenologist Michel Rolland's know-how and some of the country's best parcels of Merlot. And the result? Hammered together in true Rolland style, CA Merlot is an essay in concentration and richness. Purple in colour, this wine buzzes with sweet plum and milk chocolate, while a mouthful of dark, sweet, and inky fruit leads to a clean, dry, finish – such good value!

Thandi
Chardonnay 2004
Elgin
South Africa

get it from…
United Kingdom
£6.64

Tesco

From the moment you set foot on Thandi's Lebanon farm south of Cape Town, the immense sense of pride and passion that radiates from all involved is little short of overwhelming. And proud they should be, as in 1993 Thandi was the first winery to achieve Fairtrade accreditation, and this is a community project kicking goals for its people. Thandi Chardonnay is everything I'd hope to see from great – even pricier – New World examples: ripe stone fruit, nicely used wood – textural, long, and balanced. Hunt it down.

get it from…

United Kingdom
£19.99

Philglas & Swiggot

Meerlust
Rubicon 2001
Stellenbosch
South Africa

A visit to Meerlust – one of the most highly respected wine producers on the cape – is like a lesson in attention to detail. Displaying bucket-loads of charm, the Bordeaux-inspired Rubicon is the most serious wine in the Meerlust arsenal. The nose is rammed with tightly wound cassis and dark berry fruit alongside aromas of tobacco leaf, cedar, and sweet spice. The palate is minerally and rich, with brilliant length, flavour, and the kind of structure that's likely to see it outlive you and me!

Condado de Haza 2002
Ribera del Duero
Spain

Straight from the set of a Sergio Leone western comes Condado de Haza – well, at least the label does…. As the little brother of the iconic Pesquera, the main difference is how the wine is handled in the winery. French oak makes way for American here, and Condado is a more upfront style than its bigger sibling. Jammed with ultra-ripe, plummy fruit and a good dollop of spicy oak, this is nothing short of pure magic, especially alongside a nice rare slab of barbecued lamb.

Cono Sur Vision
Gewürztraminer 2005
Casablanca Valley
Chile

get it from…
United Kingdom
£7.99

Majestic

As far as smells and flavours go,
Gewürz should go down as one of
the more interesting grape varieties
doing the rounds. At best, it makes
wines which are incredibly
captivating, smelling so good it
sometimes seems a shame to drink
them. Oozing scents of lychee,
orange blossom, ginger, and spice,
the palate of this wine is rich and
oily with low acidity and a great
length of flavour.

Penfolds Bin 389
Cabernet/Shiraz 2002
Multi-regional blend
Australia

get it from…

United Kingdom
£15.29

Morrisons
Tesco
Sainsbury's

Much like its iconic sibling, Grange, Bin 389 also has its loyal following of fans. This Cabernet/Shiraz blend oozes smells of plum, cassis, liquorice, cedar, and freshly ground pepper. The palate is rich and seamless, with weight and intensity being the keys. The power of fruit is matched by soft acidity and firm, drying tannin – beautifully balanced, and built for the long haul. Stick it away for a while, or decant it and enjoy now.

get it from...

United Kingdom
£18.00

Majestic
Philglas & Swiggot
Selfridges

Cloudy Bay
Pelorus 2001
Marlborough
New Zealand

Unless you've been living in a
bubble, you'll know of the
phenomenon that is Cloudy Bay –
you may even have tried the wine
that started it all! But way more than
just a one-trick pony, Cloudy Bay is
also home to Pelorus, one of the
Southern Hemisphere's best
sparkling wines.

Pieced together using the traditional
method, you'll find intense lemon
citrus, cashew and spice aromas,
while the palate is rich and mouth-
filling with cleansing acidity and
great length of flavour.

United Kingdom
£9.95

Christopher Piper Wines

Fairview
Viognier 2005
Paarl
South Africa

Charles Back makes more than just a handful of great wines, but it's the ass-kickingly brilliant Viognier from this estate that excites me most. Where too many examples of this variety are guilty of being fat, rich, and overdone, Fairview's version is anything but. Aromatically, it's as you'd hope, with apricot and orange blossom leading the way. But in the mouth, it's restrained – definitely not flabby or oily – and stunning citrus/stone fruit balanced by focused acidity guides you home.

Wynns
Cabernet Sauvignon 2001
Coonawarra
Australia

get it from…

United Kingdom
£8.29

Oddbins
Majestic

From making ridiculously good
(and well-priced) Riesling to the
flagship Michael Shiraz, chief
winemaker Sue Hodder is nothing
short of a magician. Concentrated,
inky, and dense, this wine's nose is
loaded with smells of cassis, leather,
spice, and mint. The palate is
weighty and full, with heaps of fruit
and brilliant structure. Best of all, the
oak has been dealt out sparingly.
And while it provides terrific
drinking now, you could happily
stash this away for the better part
of the next decade.

TV
Dinners

Food, glorious food – and made even better by a well-chosen glass of wine. Like a romantic night in with the Mrs or Mr, food-and-wine matching shouldn't be an exercise saved only for special occasions, nor does it need to be expensive. Take some time and think about it; there's a match for just about everything. Have fun playing around with different combinations, but never let food-and-wine matching get in the way of simply enjoying something to eat and drink.

Hewitson Old Garden
Mourvèdre 2003
Barossa Valley
Australia

get it from…

United Kingdom
£16.49

Noel Young Wines

One of the brightest sparks in the Australian wine scene, Dean Hewitson is the master craftsman responsible for creating more than just a handful of brilliant wines over the course of the past decade. Sourced from mega-rare, old-vine (and we're talking over 150 years old) Mourvèdre, we're stepping into serious steak baguette with onion jam, beetroot, horseradish, and rocket territory here.

Nicolas Potel
Bourgogne Rouge 2004
Burgundy
France

get it from…
United Kingdom
£8.26

Tanners Wine Merchants

Nicolas Potel's entry-level Pinot Noir is a crystal-clear illustration of the Potel house style. And great as these wines are – particularly with anything remotely gamey – rarely, if ever, do they long for suitable matches. Think mushrooms, tuna, salmon, and duck. On the nose it's all wound up with liqueur cherry, violets, and spice, while in your mouth you'll find it's silky, fine, and balanced by some nice, dry, grippy tannin.

Licenced to Swill
Friday, 10 March 2006, 1:10pm

We're talking about a variety which, if it were a young man being taken home to meet the in-laws for the very first time – and *you* were the in-laws – you'd be very happy indeed. He'd probably drive a gleaming Aston Martin, nearly always wear a black dinner suit, and more than likely work for the secret service – not forgetting an ability to leap tall buildings in a single bound… Whoops, wrong guy.

Anyhow, bearing all the hallmarks of greatness – power, structure, focus, longevity, and an uncanny ability to travel and succeed – this is the king of all red grapes. Yep, we're talking about the 007 of the wine world; we're talking about Cabernet Sauvignon.

But a comparison with 007 might just be a tad rich, because as much as I love great Cabernet, I find more

mediocre Cabernet in my life than I'd like. Maybe that says more about me? For various reasons, Cabernet is not without its critics, but the one thing that has to be said for this variety is it's incredibly consistent. Given a bit of TLC, and Mother Nature permitting, there's no reason why you shouldn't end up with a full-bodied, cassis-laden, highly structured wine.

Predictable? Maybe. But then, so is the Bond formula: ruthless villain poses threat to world peace, only one good guy can stop him; enter all number of beautiful ladies, high-tech gadgets, and bad guys; good guy uses high-tech gadgets to beat ruthless villain/bad guys and save the world; good guy ends up with the best of the beautiful ladies. And since when did that predictable formula ever stop us coming back for more?

United Kingdom
£6.99

Adnams Wine
Merchants
Brindisa
WoodWinters Wines

Viña Rodriguez LZ
Tempranillo 2004
Rioja
Spain

Telmo Rodriguez is a man on a mission. If he's not clocking up the kilometres scouring the country in a bid to create some of the most keenly priced and exciting wines coming out of Spain, then you'll more than likely catch him studying long-range swell forecasts looking for the biggest waves he can possibly find!

Fear not: LZ isn't as adrenaline-fuelled as you might expect, nor is it as pumped up as some of its contemporaries. In both the current 04, and soon to be released 05 vintages, dark cherry and forest fruits add balance to a pretty rustic nose, while the palate is nicely knit and medium in body, making it the perfect char-grilled lamb souvlaki wine.

get it from…

United Kingdom
£7.99

Waitrose
The Wine Society

d'Arenberg The Hermit Crab
Viognier/Marsanne 2004
McLaren Vale
Australia

One of the most delicious cuts of
pork is the belly. Sure, it's fatty, but
then that's where the flavour is.
My fave is to stuff and roll a squarish
piece of belly with a mix of fresh
herbs, fennel seeds, and garlic. It
ends up roasting for about four to
five hours at a super-low heat with
continual turning and basting.
The result is magic, and you should
end up with golden, crispy skin on
the outside and sweet, gelatinous
meat within.

Full-bodied whites will do the trick
here – this concentrated and richly
textured blend from d'Arenberg is
spot on for the job.

get it from…

United Kingdom
£9.95

Roberson
The Sussex Wine
Company
The Wine Library

Nino Franco
Rustico Prosecco NV
Valdobbiadene, Veneto
Italy

Apart from the fact that it's just manners to offer your guests a drink when they arrive, a well-chosen wine should stimulate your appetite, make you hungry, and – if things are going a wee bit pear-shaped in the kitchen – buy you a bit more time. Good Prosecco is the perfect way to start, although good examples are thin on the ground. Nino Franco is the king of good Prosecco, and this wine, loaded with green apple, pear, and lemon-sherbet flavour, should be enough to have you salivating in seconds.

Wirra Wirra Mrs Wigley Rosé 2004
McLaren Vale
Australia

Fresh red fruits dominate the nose of this fuchsia-stained rosé from the stables of one of Oz's top producers, Wirra Wirra. Being light, clean, and well-structured in the mouth lends it further to a serious range of food styles and ingredients – and almost certainly guarantees it "hall of fame" status when served alongside barbecued sardines with nothing more than a pinch of sea salt and a wedge of lemon. Cheers!

get it from...

United Kingdom
£7.99

Stevens Garnier Wine Shop

Royal Tokáji
Aszú 5 Puttonyos 2000
Tokaj
Hungary

get it from...
United Kingdom
£15.99

Majestic

Chocolate and wine: two items bound not to be found together in the Gastronomic Hall of Fame. You may well know the tragic story of tricky textures, extreme sweetness – or, on the other hand, extreme bitterness – which more often than not keep these two apart. But one beacon in the midst of all that misery is Tokáji – Hungary's legendary sweet wine and brilliant partner to chocolate of the bitter kind. Relatively obscure? Yep, but totally worth the hunt.

Lawson's Dry Hills
Gewürztraminer 2004
Marlborough
New Zealand

Lawson's has been at it since 1992, and quickly developed a reputation for producing clean, well-made wines not to mention a cult-like following for its Gewürztraminer. With textbook lychee, rosewater, and musk notes, the palate, too, is rich without being fat, with good focus and balance.

If you're looking for something to eat with this and have access to decent fish, try steaming a whole snapper or sea bass together with ginger, chilli, spring onion, coriander, and soy. Delicious!

Merlonay
Friday, 11 November 2005
1:52am

Sincere apologies, but it *was 1st April*. I needed something to write about, and the notion of ancient vines found by the Mars Lunar Rover just wasn't going to cut it. And so a Skinner-dreamed genetically engineered cross between Merlot and Chardonnay – 'Merlonay' – just seemed kind of funny at the time.

The list of casualties taken in was huge, too, but there was one in particular that took the cake. Yep, there was no scalp bigger, or more personally satisfying, than that of Chris Terry's: photographer, Renaissance man, one of my best mates – a bloke who has travelled with me to nearly every wine-producing country on earth, a bloke who definitely should have known better. Surely the "looks white, tastes red – perfect for those of you who don't like the fact that red wine stains your teeth" line should have set alarm bells ringing.

But no….

And so the message left on my voicemail nearly three months after I wrote and sent the piece went something along the lines of "Skinner? Um, I'm pretty sure that I may just have fallen for another of your stupid practical jokes. I'm in Oddbins and I've just asked the guys behind the counter to recommend the best Merlonay they stock, to which they responded by erupting in fits of laughter."

The message ended along the lines of, "You're a stupid Australian and you're *not* funny."

Brilliant.

Chambers Rosewood Vineyards Rutherglen Grand Muscat NV
Rutherglen
Australia

get it from…

United Kingdom
£7.45

Lay & Wheeler

How do you best describe an Eccles cake (St John London does the best I've tried)? Think spiced dried currants, citrus peel, and burnt sugar creating a dense, golf-ball-sized filling for a buttery pastry casing. If you're not a big fan of mince pies, you probably won't like Eccles cakes much, either, but with a glass or three of Chambers Grand, now could be the perfect time to give them another look. Sporting dried raisin, *rancio*-notes, spice, spirit, and wave after wave of intensity, both the aromatics and the flavour of this wine are pure magic.

Perrin et Fils
Réserve Côtes du Rhône 2004
Southern Rhône
France

get it from…
United Kingdom
£6.99

Majestic

A Château de Beaucastel habit can be an expensive one to satisfy. Luckily for those of us who're hooked but aren't on Beaucastel-like salaries, there's the brilliant Perrin range to keep the fires burning bright. Although this isn't Beaucastel, it is great and, better still, it's affordable.

Côtes du Rhône is my idea of the perfect "one-pot dish" wine. Bright fruit, a little oak, pepper, and spice all rise to the challenge – even sing – when paired alongside something like pot-roasted lamb with Moroccan spices.

get it from…

United Kingdom
£6.99

everywine.co.uk

Brown Brothers
Tempranillo 2004
Milawa
Australia

Is there any better comfort food than sausages and mash? Don't think so. Maybe with a squeeze of roasted garlic added to the mash and a big dollop of grainy mustard on the side you could improve on it slightly, but it's pretty much perfect as it is.

Brown Brothers is one of Australia's most successful family wineries producing a range of varieties and styles across a number of regions. Alongside more internationally recognizable varieties in the camp sits this stylish Spanish ex-pat Tempranillo in which smells of cherryish fruit, tobacco, and earth combine to create a brilliant match for a TV-dinner classic.

Planeta
Chardonnay 2004
Sicily
Italy

Piping-hot oven aside, a whole chicken stuffed with lemon, butter, garlic, salt, pepper, and fresh thyme is all you need to create Chardonnay heaven.

Big but perfectly formed, Planeta Chardonnay is a full-throttle Sicilian example complete with a super-dooper grapefruit core, sweet spice, and beautifully handled oak – all of which will work to support the texture and sweetness of the meat with ease. Remember not to serve it too cold, or you'll mask all that amazing flavour.

Dr Loosen
Bernkasteler Lay Riesling
Kabinett 2004
Mosel-Saar-Ruwer
Germany

get it from…
United Kingdom
£10.99

Jeroboams

Taking the place of a traditional family roast, Sunday morning *yum cha* (dim sum to UK readers) is a regular fixture in our household. There's plenty to love about it, too: families, noise, communal eating, and – most importantly – the food.

For years I've used this weekly ritual to road-test all kinds of wine, but none have withstood the challenges of *yum cha* quite like German Riesling. Delicate, a little bit sweet, pure, and lime-edged, this example from one of the world's great white winemakers, Ernst Loosen, is way more than just worthy of your attention.

Skin Deep
Friday, 10 March 2006, 2:42pm

A few years back, a mate of mine headed to Spain for "a week away with the boys". A couple of days into the blur, a few of them decided that souvenir tattoos might be a good idea. And so off they went. You already know this is going to be bad, don't you!

Terry, my mate, decided he'd have his own name tattooed on his arm (I put that down to drinking) – to this day, he remembers very little about having the tattoo done (I put that down to the drinking, too). So imagine his surprise when, the following morning, complete with raging hangover, he gets out of bed, shoulder throbbing, only to catch a glimpse of his brand-new tattoo in the mirror for the very first time: "BERRY". Seriously!

Packaging can make or break a wine. The sheer amount of bad wine that's overcompensated for by pumped-up packaging is dizzying. But, that said, plenty of us still make purchases based on nothing more than aesthetics. Some go by the amount of medals on the front of the bottle. Medals count for little – particularly when they were won at "Uncle Bob's Backyard Wine Show".

The other packaging tool we rely on far too much is the back label. Always bear in mind that a back label is never going to tell you how bad a wine is. The other fatal misconception is bottle weight and its effect on quality: the heavier the bottle, the better the wine. God, if only that were true! The only thing that you should be concerned with on a wine bottle is the name of the producer: it counts for absolutely everything.

As they say, beauty is only skin deep. And luckily for Terry, it's what's inside that really counts!

Craggy Range
Te Muna Road Vineyard
Pinot Noir 2004
Martinborough
New Zealand

get it from...

United Kingdom
£14.99

Waitrose

Sometimes some of the most satisfying meals are the ones that take the least amount of time and effort. If I can't face cooking dinner, I'll often pick up half a Chinese roast duck and some steamed jasmine rice. And to drink? Pinot Noir. Pinot and duck share another of those spiritual food-and-wine relationships.

Apart from being insanely good value, this wine is all wound up with liqueur-cherry, violet, and spice aromas such as cinnamon, nutmeg, and clove. Once in your mouth you'll find it is silky, fine, and balanced by some nice, dry, grippy tannin – perfect for navigating sweet and sticky duck.

Shaw & Smith
M3 Vineyard Chardonnay 2004
Adelaide Hills
Australia

Among the examples currently flying the flag for Australia's new breed of Chardonnay, Shaw & Smith M3 is a very deliberate attempt to create pure, textured, age-worthy Chardonnay that you don't need to use a knife and fork on. Controlled and elegant, M3 lends itself to a broad range of food styles, but in order to save you time, you could do a whole lot worse than a couple of big, fat char-grilled pork chops, a dollop of salsa verde, and some boiled new potatoes. Delicious.

United Kingdom
£15.55

Gauntleys of Nottingham

Lustau
San Emilio Pedro Ximénez NV
Jerez
Spain

This is an absolute no-brainer, and your guests/better half is going to love you for it! Grab a tub of rum-and-raisin ice-cream (vanilla if you're a purist), place two scoops in a bowl, and pour "PX" liberally over the top as though it were hot chocolate sauce. Bingo: you have an instant killer dessert.

Lustau PX is perhaps the finest sherry produced in Jerez. Olive-mahogany to look at, on the nose it's all molasses, dried raisins, spice, and spirit, while in the mouth it's syrupy, rich, clean, and long.

Finders Keepers
Friday, 31 March 2006, 12:24pm

Never before have I paid such close attention to a vintage as I have done this year. I've literally got everything crossed for a textbook 2006 harvest. I tell you, this one counts like no other – well, it does for me, anyway.

My concern/anticipation stems from the fact that I'm looking for something to lay down for when my newly-born daughter, Indi, is older. Sort of selfishly, I'm already thinking about Riesling and Pinot Noir – not just because these are two of my favourite varieties, but because benchmark examples possess an uncanny ability to age like few other varieties.

While young Riesling is all about purity and structure, these are the very same things that will help them develop into citrus-rich, kerosene-tinged, old-age rippers. The best examples of Pinot Noir, on the other hand, generally go from being simple, primary-fruit-driven wines to lush, velvety, and seductive – still fruit-driven examples, only with a nice savoury edge to them that just unfolds from the moment you pull the cork or open the cap.

In any case, we're talking about two varieties that inspire you to hang on to and lay down a few bottles for a rainy day somewhere along the line. And while I acknowledge that everybody's motivation for drinking wine is different, both Riesling and Pinot Noir are the reasons that I, and hoards of other freaks like me, love and keep wine.

Pewsey Vale
Riesling 2004
Eden Valley
Australia

get it from...

United Kingdom
£8.99

Oz Wines
Theatre of Wine
Vin du Van

Like Vegemite, Dunlop Volleys and Harold Bishop, Pewsey Vale Riesling is iconically Australian. Lime-scented, ripe, and floral, this is classic Eden Valley Riesling and remains one of Australia's greatest bargain wine buys.

And so whether you don't feel much like cooking, or you're just plain rubbish in the kitchen, a bottle of Pewsey Vale Riesling firmly tucked under one arm and a bag full of fresh Vietnamese rice-paper rolls in the other will have you eating and drinking in true style.

get it from…

United Kingdom
£14.95

Bennett's Wine Merchants

Fèlsina Berardenga
Chianti Classico 2003
Tuscany
Italy

Sangiovese, Tuscany's native red superstar, never makes more sense than with food. Naturally high in tannin, these wines can be hard work on their own, but paired with the right kind of food – meat, pasta or anything a little bit fatty – and you'll struggle to find a better match.

Fèlsina Chianti Classico comes sporting a solid core of pure, dark, cherryish fruit alongside smells of tobacco, leather, earth, and spice. In the mouth it's minerally, rich, and rounded out by a wash of trademark dry, grippy Sangiovese tannin. *Bellissimo!*

get it from…

United Kingdom
£11.99

Selfridges

Chapel Down
Brut NV
Kent
England

I know it seems posh, but it really is such a lovely combo. We're talking about freshly shucked oysters (with nothing more than a small squeeze of lemon) paired up with a glass of fizz – in this case, bubbles from one of England's finest producers. Hammered together from the traditional Champagne varieties, Chapel Down has skilfully created a wine that well and truly over-delivers for the money. Shock your doubting friends with how brilliant this wine is!

Bonny Doon
Le Cigare Volant 2003
Central Coast
California

get it from…

United Kingdom
£25.95

Berry Bros & Rudd

PRODUCER OF THE YEAR

Lovingly assembled by one of our favourite characters, Randall Grahm's homage to the absurdity that saw flying saucers banned from landing in Châteauneuf-du-Pape during the 1950s is little short of pure magic. The tongue-in-cheek tone is set with the packaging, but the wine couldn't be any more serious.

Take a big sniff and find a solid core of blackcurrant, plum, and raspberry fruit alongside liquorice, leather, and ground coffee. The palate is chewy and dense, big but beautiful. You're going to need some serious meat here!

Iona
Sauvignon Blanc 2005
Elgin
South Africa

get it from…

United Kingdom
£11.25

Philglas & Swiggot

When I die, I really hope that I come
back as the son of a Mexican chef.
A family restaurant somewhere
around Todos Santos would be a
massive bonus, but I'm not fussy.
You see, I love Mexican food – not
Tex-Mex, but proper authentic
Mexican food. At this point you
could probably opt for margaritas or
beer as the drink of choice, but
fortunately that's not an option here!
Fresh, fruit-driven whites – without
the use of oak – will serve you well.

Suckfizzle
Cabernet Sauvignon 2002
Margaret River
Australia

get it from…

United Kingdom
£16.00

Oddbins
Falernian Fine Wines
Swig Wine Merchants

Lamb and Cabernet Sauvignon share an amazing relationship, and definitely rank among food and wine's all-time classic matches. In the case of Janice McDonald's slick Margaret River example, sweet, blackcurrant- and plum-driven fruit stack up nicely to the sweetness of the meat, while dry, grippy tannin works to break down protein and cut through fat. Slow-roasted shoulder (rather than the more expensive leg) of lamb surrounded by veg is a bit of a staple in our house – and this wine is the perfect partner here.

get it from…

United Kingdom
£5.99

Sainsbury's

Barbadillo
Solear Manzanilla NV
Sanlúcar de Barrameda
Spain

Manzanilla sherry is one of the greatest food wines produced anywhere in the world. Like this baby here, the best examples of manzanilla are bone-dry, nutty, and slightly salty with an awesome minerally tang. These wines rise to the occasion beautifully when paired with foods such as olives, anchovies, capers, cured meats, and nuts.

As a point of interest, manzanilla is best drunk fresh off the boat (ask your retailer) and should be served chilled. Buying half-bottles will further maximize the freshness, too.

Chrismont
Riesling 2005
King Valley
Australia

I love Malaysian, Hawker-style food. Soup-based *laksas* are a favourite: sweet, creamy coconut soup creates the tangy base in which a raw hit of chilli, a squeeze of fresh lime juice, punchy coriander, snap-fresh bean sprouts, rice vermicelli, fat, juicy prawns, squid, and fish cake all play a part.

So what do you drink with this? Riesling! Chrismont, one of the most well-respected producers in Victoria's King Valley, produces a rich, dry, and limey style that stacks up perfectly to this challenging but delicious combo of texture and flavour.

Saint Clair
Sauvignon Blanc 2005
Marlborough
New Zealand

The smell of spring in the air should have you automatically reaching for Sauvignon Blanc. This season's ingredients are literally made for this variety! Pure gooseberry and blackcurrant fruit lay the foundation for another mouth-watering Matt Thomson wine – this year in the form of the stunning Saint Clair Sauvignon Blanc.

One final tip on a food match: broad beans, peas, mint, basil, lemon, sea salt, good oil, and parmesan pounded up in a pestle and mortar and spread on toast. Trust me…

Bling

Welcome to the section of the guide where we throw caution to the wind and bravely show the budget the door. For what it's worth, our bling isn't all about what it cost, but rather, what it's *worth*. For many different reasons, these are some of our all-time favourite bottles. Remember that with wine you generally get what you pay for, and in the case of the following wines, mega-attention to detail, tiny productions, and well-earned reputations count for everything.

get it from…

United Kingdom
£15.95

Lea & Sandeman

The Escarpment
Pinot Noir 2004
Martinborough
New Zealand

NZ legend Larry McKenna's quest to produce high-quality Pinot Noir from his Escarpment project has been duly rewarded here with his killer third release. Concentrated and perfumed, this wine displays a tightly-wound core of plum and dark forest fruit underpinned by hints of earth and spice, not to mention some deftly handled cedary oak. The palate is generous, silky and long, and in a couple of words, the bomb.

Moët et Chandon
Cuvée Dom Pérignon 1998
Champagne
France

get it from…

United Kingdom
£89.00

Harrods
Lea & Sandeman
Selfridges

Named in honour of the monk of
the same name. If ever there was
a wine that has become
synonymous with bling, then
surely it's Dom Pérignon. But is
it really worth the money?
Absolutely. It's like a great big
jigsaw puzzle: the team at
Moët assembles this wine from
a selection of the very best parcels
of Pinot Noir and Chardonnay from
across the best vineyards. The
selection process is ruthless. The
result is breathtaking.

Felton Road
Block 5 Pinot Noir 2004
Central Otago
New Zealand

get it from...

United Kingdom
£32.95

Averys Wine
Merchants

Otago is the furthest point south of the equator that you could wish to grow grapes. Unique inland micro-climates create pockets of warmth which, aided by long sunshine hours, provide the perfect environment for varieties that thrive in marginal climates. Enter Pinot Noir. Pinot has been chugging away in Central Otago for the best part of the last decade, and Felton Road is right up the pointy end of the region's top producers.

This wine is jammed full of seductive fruit and spice smells – the palate, too, is velvety and long, with fine yet firm tannins and an incredible length of flavour.

Tenuta San Guido
Sassicaia 2002
Tuscany
Italy

So there he is: the Jimmy Page and all of a sudden as I hand him the wine list I'm more nervous than when I served Jancis Robinson. As I go to speak, my voice breaks like I'm 12 again. Tenuta San Guido is home to one of the most sought-after and much-loved wines on the planet: Sassicaia – a Cabernet-based blend that was originally produced to satisfy the Marquis Mario Incisa della Rocchetta's taste for Bordeaux-style wine.

Intense cherry, liquorice, and leather dominate the nose, while in the mouth it's structured, tannic, and perfectly judged. My prized bottle of Sassicaia reads: "To Matt, Rock On! Jimmy Page".

Sea Change
Friday, 3 February 2006, 1:40pm

White wine with fish, right? Sure. If I were the kind of guy who enjoyed watching test patterns and paint drying, then good old-fashioned white wine with fish would be just fine, thanks.

But I'm not.

The sea is home to a whole stack of things that require you to step outside the box and simply think beyond white wine. Take oysters, for example: they're great with Chablis, but never better than with good fizz.

And how about sherry? Forget Nana's drinks tray; sherry is back! At one end of the sherry scale lies manzanilla: a bone-dry, light, salty, slightly tangy style of wine that is simply built for basking in the sun and feasting on snap-fried calamari with garlic and char-grilled prawns.

Rosé is another wine style that will stand you in great stead with a whole range of seafood, but think barbecued sardines, squeeze of lemon, nice tunes, sunny day, and you may just have found that rare food-and-wine paradise.

And finally, how about trying on red variety Pinot Noir for size? Hang on – you can't do red with fish, can you? Yep, you sure can, but you do need to tread with care. With salmon and tuna sharing the crown for meatiest members of the fish family, Pinot Noir should nearly always be your first stop when looking for a match.

Boekenhoutskloof
Syrah 2003
Franschhoek
South Africa

Marc Kent is the man responsible for the insanely good Boekenhoutskloof range. Obsessed with the Rhône, Kent has fashioned Old World ideas together with some of South Africa's finest fruit.

This wine is of sumo proportions and has been built for the long haul. It has semi-trailer loads of fruit, with smoked meat, spice, and cedar smells. The palate is rich, concentrated, and long, with sweet, persistent fruit, great balance, and firm but stealth-like tannin.

Giaconda
Chardonnay 2004
Beechworth
Australia

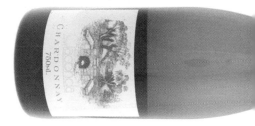

get it from…

United Kingdom
£50

Philglas & Swiggot

Giaconda is now something of
a legend. Not only does Rick
Kinzbrunner's Chardonnay rank
among the world's best (cue Euro-
centric purists soiling their pinstripes
in horror over that statement), but it
is arguably Australia's finest.

We're talking about an incredibly
rich and textural wine where
restrained grapefruit and nectarine-
like fruit take centre stage alongside
scents of fresh toast, grilled hazelnut,
and pork rind. The palate is long,
rich, minerally, and lush. Swap vital
organs for some if you have to.

F X Pichler
Riesling Smaragd
Von den Terrassen 2004
Wachau
Austria

FX Pichler's wines are like
M C Escher drawings: elaborate,
linear, intricate, precise, a little bit
mathematical, but above all else,
captivating. Add to that smells and
flavours of fresh lime juice, green
apples, minerals, and spice and
suddenly you get sexy, too.

If ever you need convincing (or
need to convince another) that
Riesling can perhaps stake a claim
to being the world's greatest white
grape variety, then this is your
trump card. Play it with pride!

Nyetimber
Classic Cuvée 1998
West Sussex
England

get it from…

United Kingdom
£22.50

Harvey Nichols
Majestic

It looks like it, smells like it, tastes like it – it's even made like it – but it ain't Champagne. It's just good old sparkling wine from England. In fact, that sells it short, because Nyetimber is better than just "good": it's really, *really* good.

Planted on the chilly chalk escarpments of West Sussex and drawing on the traditional Champagne varieties of Pinot Noir, Chardonnay, and Pinot Meunier, this is England's best example of sparkling wine. It scores Rolls Royce treatment in the winery, too, and as a result has developed a cult-like following of fans which, apart from us, is even said to include H.R.H.

Bollinger
La Grande Année 1997
Champagne
France

Bollinger is well-known for producing a complex and powerful style of fizz, thanks to extended lees-ageing and the clever use of oak. And while these wines are generally built to go the distance, the good news for us is that the sun-soaked 1997 Grande Année is ready to drink now. Scents of Pinot Noir fruit and freshly toasted brioche set you up for a mouthful of rich stone/citrus fruit that's creamy and direct, with firm acidity and an incredible length of flavour. A genuine jaw-dropper from one of Champagne's greatest houses.

Finders Keepers – Part Two
Friday, 7 April 2006, 12:50pm

Shortly after landing my first job in the wine trade, one of my closest mates turned 21. I thought a bottle of something really special – something he could lay down for decades to come – would be a fitting way to mark the occasion. Penfolds Grange 1991 was just out, and so, taking into consideration my staff discount (together with how little I knew about the value of what I was buying), I settled on a bottle of Australia's most iconic wine as the perfect gift for a 21-year-old whose main interests included sex, drugs and rock 'n' roll....

He was stoked with the gesture, too, but his dad, a big wine-lover, was horrified – with good reason. The problem was that Matt lived in the kind of student commune that made *Animal House* look like *The Good Life*. For years the bottle lived at the back of his wardrobe, escaping the clutches of many a 4am session, until one morning when, much to Matt's horror, he returned home just in time to find one of his housemates just starting to lever the cork from the bottle…

Short of owning a cellar (and that's most of us, I suspect), there are three things you should be aware of if you're planning to stick a few bottles down. Excessive light, vibration, and dramatic fluctuations of temperature are all no-no's. Find a cool, dark place: a cupboard is fine so long as a) it's not also home to the hot-water service and b) it has a lock.

You might be pleased to know that it was a happy ending. To this day, that bottle of Grange 1991 remains unopened and is now safely tucked away from the threat of any student house.

Crawford River
Riesling 2004
Condah Valley
Australia

get it from…

United Kingdom
£13.00

Justerini & Brooks

Schinnnngggg! Remember that sword sound effect you hear in martial-arts films? If I had to use a sound to describe this wine, then that'd have to be it. Since the mid-1970s, John Thomson has been carving out amazingly rich, pure, and steely examples of Riesling, many of which will long outlive you and me. Dominated by focused, limey fruit and razor-sharp acidity, these are wines that are super-well-defined and beautifully balanced.

Dominio de Pingus
Flor de Pingus 2003
Ribera del Duero
Spain

get it from…

United Kingdom
£31.41

Corney & Barrow

Sounds a bit like something I'd make up (à la "Merlonay"), but the Pingus rise to superstardom came as the result of a bizarre shipping disaster. That's not to say that Pingus wasn't already on the way up (it was); this just made it happen a little quicker… And so when 200 cases of Pingus 1997 were lost somewhere off the Atlantic coast, both price and demand skyrocketed. Peter Sisseck knows Ribera del Duero inside out, and by way of contrast, Pingus is much more modern than nearby neighbour Vega Sicilia, and with the brilliant 04 vintage just available. Check them both out.

get it from…

United Kingdom
£85.00

Roberson Wine Merchants
Vinoteca

Château Ducru-Beaucaillou St-Julien 2000 (Deuxième Cru)
Bordeaux
France

Unlike neighbouring Pauillac, the commune of St-Julien has no First Growths to brag about, but that's certainly not to say that it has no stars. DB is perhaps St-Julien's most loyal soldier. As a consistently muscular blend of mainly Cabernet Sauvignon and Merlot, it is built to go the distance.

The 2000 vintage shows all the signs of being a classic. And while the price tag might be enough to get your heart racing, by Bordeaux standards this wine still represents amazing value for money.

Château d'Yquem
Lur-Saluces Sauternes 1999
(Premier Cru Supérieur)
Bordeaux
France

get it from…

United Kingdom
£100.00

Uncorked
Vinoteca

By Westwood standards, Château d'Yquem is the big dog of Sauternes. Head and shoulders above the rest of the pack in terms of both quality and price, d'Yquem employs one of the strictest quality regimes of any wine producer anywhere on the planet. And the result is enough to make your eyes water. Punchy citrus marmalade, sun-soaked apricot, sweet spice, and deftly used new oak is what you'll find here, all of which is orchestrated by incredible balance and length. Keep an eye out for the mind-blowing 2001 vintage. Rare but worth the hunt. Holler!

Moss Wood
Cabernet Sauvignon 2000
Margaret River
Australia

In a region that's not light on stars, Moss Wood sits happily at the top of Margaret River's distinguished heap. Here you'll find a nose layered with tightly wound cassis and dark berry fruit alongside scents of liquorice, leather, and wild mint. The palate is an essay in concentration, with focused fruit, a mineral-like texture, and measured, dry, grippy tannin. The application of a screwcap to a percentage of one of Australia's most iconic wines only adds to the big smiles already gracing our faces!

Domaine Armand Rousseau
Gevrey-Chambertin
Clos St-Jacques 1997
Burgundy
France

Chances are that if you're a keen fan of Burgundy, you'll already know of the exquisite Domaine Armand Rousseau. You may even have had the good fortune (and the cash) to have tasted a few of the wines. If not, listen up, as Pinot Noir doesn't get much better than this.

In essence, the wines of Rousseau are all about purity and finesse. And while the equation of old vines, low yields, and wines moved only by gravity might not sound like anything new to Burgundy-lovers, the end result is wines that are multi-layered, super-silky, incredibly pure, and little short of magic.

Bellavista
Cuvée Brut NV
Lombardy
Italy

Bellavista is one of the best sparkling wines outside of the Champagne region in France. Hailing from Franciacorta in Italy's northeastern corner, Bellavista is a blend of Chardonnay, Pinot Noir (here called "Pinot Nero"), and Pinot Bianco. The wine smells of citrus fruit, restrained stone fruits, and honeysuckle, while the palate is rich and focused, with a superfine bead and great length. Perfect pre-dinner or with lighter seafood dishes.

get it from…
United Kingdom

Berry Bros & Rudd
£782.98 (150 cl magnum)

Majestic
£400 (75cl bottle)

Château Pétrus
Pomerol 1993
Bordeaux
France

At around £400 a bottle I really
should have known better. Thank
you, Gordon Ramsay…
Brick/garnet to look at, this is
aromatically really subdued with a
solid, but ultra-tightly wound core of
cassis, cedar, and spice. To say it's a
touch rustic wouldn't have been out
of line. But once tasted, I knew I was
in trouble. This was *good* – really,
really good. Rich and expansive,
with masses of dark Merlot fruit that
just unwound in your mouth, terrific
mineral intensity, and punctuated
by a wash of superfine tannin… this
could only have been great
Bordeaux. And it is.

Hot Food, Cool Wine
Friday, 30 September 2005
3:02pm

Matching wine to Chinese food defies convention – and I love that. In a world full of rules and regulations, the fact that you can just toss the rulebook out the window and start from scratch is a breath of fresh air. Look at the foundations of each dish; from experience, I've found that wines which can handle at least two or three of these key cornerstones – sweet, sour, salty, and hot – will serve you best.

Sadly, Champagne and sparkling wine's overall compatibility with Chinese cooking is all too brief for me, but where most bubbles struggle, sparkling red reigns supreme. Texture is the key here, with high-acid fizz providing a brilliant vehicle for cleaning your palate of fat and/or salt. With most fizzy reds sporting a hint of sweetness and just a dash of tannin, these are wines that should work brilliantly with anything sweet, sour, hot, and/or sticky.

Aromatic whites are worth a go, too, but none stack up quite like Riesling. And Riesling, particularly the Germanic style, has it all. Delicate fruit flavours, low alcohol, lively acidity, and a touch of residual sugar will rise to the challenge when paired with all manner of steamed and fried dumplings, glutinous rice, slippery hand-stretched noodles, and a cast of sauces.

Pinot Noir and duck aside (one of the world's great wine and food combinations) reds can be very tricky. And although star-studded line-ups of full-bodied whites and reds adorn Chinese wine lists aplenty rarely do they fit the bill, due to excessive amounts of flavour, alcohol, and in the case of reds, tannin.

Cloudy Bay
Sauvignon Blanc 2005
Marlborough
New Zealand

get it from…

United Kingdom
£16.00

Selfridges
Philglas & Swiggot

Each year the first wines to hit our shelves are usually those which require the smallest amount of TLC during production – white variety Sauvignon Blanc is a classic example. Responsible for fuelling the global love affair with New Zealand Sauvignon Blanc, Cloudy Bay is the original article, and while wines from this estate get tougher to lay your hands on by the second, the quality is without question, and they remain at the top of the tree.

True to form, the 2005 is a classic: full of explosive gooseberry, elderflower, and blackcurrant slung together with mouth-watering acidity.

Didier Dagueneau
Silex Pouilly-Fumé 2004
Loire Valley
France

get it from…
United Kingdom
£67.50

Berry Bros & Rudd

Sorry, but did you say £65 for good old Sauv Blanc? Yep, sure did! But this ain't just any good old Sauv Blanc – no, sir. This is Sauv Blanc from another galaxy…

Didier Dagueneau is unrelenting in his pursuit of quality. Vineyards are only worked by horses, and biodynamic practices have been in full effect here since 1993.

Single-vineyard, barrel-fermented, lees-aged, and little short of intergalactic, Silex might not be Sauvignon Blanc as we know it, captain, but *@&%, it's good!

get it from…

United Kingdom
£22.09

Andrew Chapman Fine
Wines

**Yering Station
Shiraz/Viognier Reserve 2003**
Yarra Valley
Australia

Good Shiraz/Viognier blends are fast becoming commonplace in Oz, while the really great examples require you to look a bit harder. The heart-stoppingly good Yering Station Reserve Shiraz Viognier is a ripper – especially when you consider both price and quality.

Solid colour and explosive aromatics coupled with medium-bodied ripe, round, spicy fruit, and fresh acidity all combine to reinforce why Tom Carson – the man behind the controls at Yering – was named International Winemaker of the Year in 2004.

Domaine Zind Humbrecht
Hengst
Gewürztraminer 2003
Alsace
France

get it from…

United Kingdom
£37.00

Berry Bros & Rudd

Olivier Humbrecht carves out some of the most insanely pure, rich, and expressive wines to be found anywhere in Alsace. Serious attention to detail in the vineyard (super-high-density planting, mega-low yields) result in wines which simply ooze varietal expression without compromising on terroir.

White peach, musk, and spice make way for a lush and silky mouthful of fruit. Just off-dry, but balanced beautifully by trademark fresh acidity.

Roberto Voerzio
Barolo La Serra 2001
Piedmont
Italy

Handcrafted by Roberto Voerzio, arguably one of the Italian wine scene's brightest stars, with a reputation for "no compromise" (which extends to one of the biggest sound systems I can ever remember seeing in a winery). This 100 per cent single-vineyard Nebbiolo has all the hallmarks of Voerzio's Midas touch. On board you'll find morello cherry, rose petals, black olives, rosemary, tobacco, exotic spice, and just the faintest whiff of Led Zeppelin. Barolo doesn't get much better than this.

get it from...

United Kingdom
£20.50

Philglas & Swiggot

Charles Melton
Nine Popes 2002
Barossa Valley
Australia

We're convinced Barossa legend Charlie Melton is the original star of the Victoria Bitter ads (the resemblance is uncanny). But as to whether Charlie really can pull large trucks out of quarries, round up cattle on horseback, and still find time to do the washing up, we may have to ask wife Virginia. One thing we are sure of, though, is just how good this man's wines are.

Charlie Melton's tongue-in-cheek homage to Châteauneuf-du-Pape ("New house of the pope") is a rich and spicy mix of old-vine, dry-grown Barossa Grenache and Shiraz (no Mourvèdre in 2002) that ropes together concentrated, dark, sweet fruit, a touch of earth and spice, and sparingly handled cedary oak.

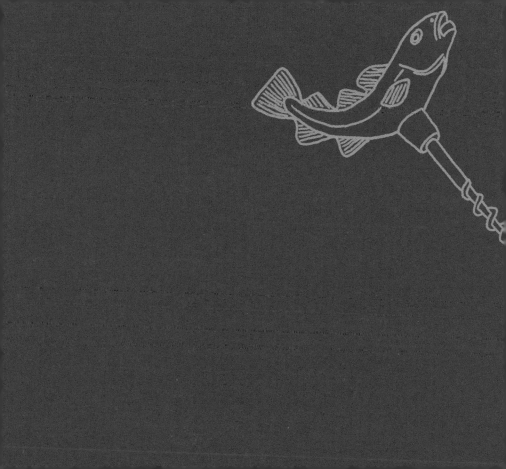

Domaine Leroy
Vosne-Romanée
Les Beaux Monts 1989
Burgundy
France

get it from…

United Kingdom
£200.00

John Armit Wines

What do you write about a domaine such as Leroy in less than 100 words? It's pretty much impossible. The story of the domaine's proprietor Madame Lalou Bize-Leroy (former co-proprietor of Domaine de la Romanée-Conti and a fierce stickler for detail) is the stuff of legends. One hundred per cent biodynamic, Leroy's wines are the very essence of what I love about Pinot Noir: multi-tiered, purely fruited, slightly animal, textural, seductive, fine, and complete.

If you ever happen to find yourself with the opportunity to taste wines from this domaine, then sell vital organs to do so. *Reeeeespect!*

Allegrini
Amarone della Valpolicella Classico 2001
Veneto
Italy

Producing great Amarone is a tough assignment. To give you the low-down, ripe grapes are harvested and then stored in a well-ventilated environment to dry for anywhere up to four months, the end product being something halfway between a grape and a raisin. At this point, freshly harvested grapes are crushed and the juice is left to ferment over the now partly dried fruit.

The results are spellbinding. Allegrini produces a clean, deeply concentrated, modern style of Amarone where ripe plum and cherry combine with dried fruit, spice, and a bitter-chocolate character.

Stockists A–Z

Adnams Wine Merchants
www.adnamswines.co.uk
01502 727222
Hugel, Viña Rodriguez

Andrew Chapman Fine Wines
www.surf4wine.co.uk
01235 821539
Yering Station

John Armit Wines
www.armit.co.uk
020 7908 0600
Domaine Leroy Vosne-Romanée;
Donny Goodmac; Yarra Yarra

Asda
www.asda-beerwinesspirits.co.uk
Michel Laroche

Averys Wine Merchants
www.averys.com
08451 283 797
Felton Road; Saint Clair

Bedales
www.bedalestreet.com
020 7403 8853
Yarra Burn

Bennetts Fine Wine Merchants
www.bennettsfinewines.com
01386 840392
Fèlsina Berardenga

Berry Bros & Rudd
www.bbr.com
0870 900 4300
Bollinger; Bonny Doon; Château
Pétrus; Didier Dagueneau;
Domaine Zind-Humbrecht;

Booths Supermarkets
www.booths-supermarkets.co.uk
Casa Lapostolle; Springfield Estate

Brindisa
www.brindisa.com
020 8772 1600
Viña Rodriguez

Cellarmarque
www.cellarmarque.co.uk
Innocent Bystander

Christopher Keiller Fine Wines
www.gladys.demon.co.uk/
finewineservices.html
01209 215716
Charles Melton

Christopher Piper Wines
01404 814139
Fairview

Connolly's Wine Merchants Ltd
www.connollyswine.co.uk
0121 236 9269
Shaw & Smith

Cooden Cellars
www.coodencellars.co.uk
01323 649663
Dr. Unger

Co-op Stores
www.coop.co.uk
Argento

Corney & Barrow
www.corneyandbarrow.com
020 7265 2400
Dominio de Pingus

deFine Food & Wine
www.definefoodandwine.com
01606 882101
Innocent Bystander

Eagle's Wines
020 7223 7209
Bay of Fires Tigress

everywine.co.uk
www.everywine.co.uk
0800 072 0011
Bellavista; Brown Brothers

Falernian Fine Wines
www.falernianwines.co.uk
01443 422608
Suckfizzle

Fareham Wine Cellar
www.farehamwinecellar.co.uk
01329 822733
Jacob's Creek

Fine & Rare Wines Ltd
www.frw.co.uk
020 8960 1995
Alain Graillot; F X Pichler; Joseph
Drouhin

Gauntleys of Nottingham
www.gauntley-wine.co.uk
0115 911 0555
Lustau

Hanslope Wines
www.hanslopewines.demon.co.uk
01908 510262
Saint Clair

Harrods
www.harrods.com
020 7730 1234
Casa Lapostolle; Moët et Chandon

Harvey Nichols
www.harveynichols.com
020 7235 5000
Boekenhoutskloof; Kumeu River;
Nyetimber

Imbibros
www.imbibros.co.uk
01483 861 164
Masi Tupungato

Jeroboams
www.jeroboams.co.uk
020 7727 9359
Dr Loosen; Moss Wood

J T Davies & Sons Ltd.
www.jtdavies.co.uk
020 8760 0390
Evans & Tate

Justerini & Brooks
www.justerinis.com
020 7484 6400
Crawford River

Lay & Wheeler
www.laywheeler.com
01473 313233
Chambers Rosewood Vineyards;
Lawson's Dry Hills

Lea and Sandeman
www.londonfinewine.co.uk
020 7244 0522
Moët et Chandon; Escarpment

Liberty Wines
www.libertywine.co.uk
020 7720 5350
Colonia Las Liebres

Luvians The Bottle Shop
www.luvians.com
01334 654 820
Innocent Bystander; Springfield
Estate

Magnum Fine Wines
www.magnum.co.uk
020 7839 5732
Springfield Estate

Majestic
www.majestic.co.uk
0845 605 6767
(Minimum purchase of 12 bottles)
Chateau Petrus; Cloudy Bay; Clos de
los Siete; Concha y Toro; Cono Sur;
Dominio de Pingus; Ermita Veracruz;
Nyetimber; Penfolds; Perrin et Fils;
Royal Tokáji; Sassicaia; Wynns

Mill Hill Wines
www.millhillwines.com
020 8959 6754
Masi Tupungato

Morrisons
www.morrisons.co.uk
0845 611 6111
Penfolds, Torres

Noel Young Wines
www.nywines.co.uk
01223 844744
Condado de Haza; Cosme
Palacio y Hermanos; Hewitson
Old Garden; Seppelt

Oddbins
www.oddbins.com
0800 917 4093
Casa Silva Doña Dominga;
Chapoutier; Concha y Toro;
Condado de Haza; Cosme
Palacio; Montana Reserve; Peter
Lehmann; Pol Roger; Seppelt;
Suckfizzle; Wynns

Olivers Wines & Spirits
www.oliverswines.co.uk
01376 571860
Yalumba "Y" Series

The Oxford Wine Company
www.oxfordwine.co.uk
01865 30 11 44
Quinta de la Rosa

Oz Wines
www.ozwines.co.uk
0845 450 1261
Pewsey Vale

Philglas & Swiggot
www.philglas-swiggot.co.uk
020 8332 6031
Charles Melton; Cloudy Bay;
Domaine Armand Rousseau;
Evans & Tate; Giaconda; Grosset;
Iona; Meerlust; Planeta

The Revelstoke Wine Co.
www.revelstoke.co.uk
0208 545 0077
Yarra Burn

Roberson Wine Merchant
www.robersonwinemerchant.co.uk
0207 371 2121
Château Ducru-Beaucaillou;
Nino Franco; Yalumba

Rodney Densem
www.rodneydensemwines.com
01270 212200
Evans & Tate

Sainsburys
www.sainsburys.co.uk
0800 636262
Argento; Barbadillo;
Boekenhoutskloof; Penfolds;
Peter Lehmann; Torres

Savage Selection
www.savageselection.co.uk
01451 860896
Yarra Burn

Selfridges & Co.
www.selfridges.com
08708 377 377
Antinori; Chapel Down; Cloudy
Bay; Masi Tupungato; Moët et
Chandon; Yalumba "Y" Series

Soho Wine Supply
www.sohowine.co.uk
020 7636 8490
Bay of Fires Tigress; Yarra Burn;

Somerfield
www.somerfield.co.uk
Boekenhoutskloof; Cono Sur

Stevens Garnier
www.stevensgarnier.co.uk
01865 263 300
Wirra Wirra Mrs Wigley

Sussex Wine Company
www.thesussexwinecompany.
co.uk 08000 272 272
Nino Franco

Swig
www.swig.co.uk
08000 272 272
Suckfizzle

Tanners Wines Merchants
www.tanners-wines.co.uk
01743 23 44 55
Nicolas Potel

Tesco
www.tesco.com
Argento; Brown Brothers; Jacob's Creek;
Penfolds; Peter Lehmann; Thandi

Thameside Wines
www.thamesidewines.com
020 8788 4752
Allegrini

The Sussex Wine Company
www.thesussexwinecompany.co.uk
01323 431143
Nino Franco

The Wine Library
www.winelibrary.co.uk
020 7481 0415
Nino Franco

The Wine Society
www.thewinesociety.com
01438 740222
Casa Lapostolle; d'Arenberg

The Wine Treasury
www.winetreasury.com
020 7793 9999
Roberto Voerzio

Theatre of Wine
www.theatreofwine.com
020 8858 6363
Pewsey Vale

Thresher Group
www.victoriawine.co.uk
01707 387 200
Hardys Oomoo

Uncorked
www.uncorked.co.uk
020 7638 5998
Château d'Yquem

Unwined
www.unwined-online.co.uk
01949 844324
Plantagenet Hazard Hill

Vin du Van
01233 758727
Pewsey Vale

Vinoteca
www.vinoteca.co.uk
020 7253 8786
Château Ducru-Beaucaillou;
Château d'Yquem; Kumeu River

Vinum
www.vinum.co.uk
020 8847 4699
Donnafugata

Waitrose
www.waitrose.com
0800 188 884
Cono Sur; Craggy Range;
d'Arenberg

Wimbledon Wine Cellar
020 8540 9979
Kumeu River

Wine Buy The Case
www.winebuythecase.com
Antinori; Michel Laroche

Woodwinters Wines & Whiskies
www.woodwinters.com
01786 834 894
Viña Rodriguez

Index

Cheers

For Carls & Indi – my two beautiful girls xx

Matt Utber, Jade, Rich, Brad and all the crew down at The Plant for once again making it look flash! Chris Terry and Danny for giving it life with yet more awesome pics. Lisa Sullivan and Esther Philip-Clunis at Fresh Partners for endless hard work, support and having to put up with me day in day out! Paul 'Magnet' Green – my right hand man for amazing loyalty and support. Xabi and Jules, Fifteen London, Cornwall, Amsterdam and Melbourne. Alison Goff, David Lamb, Fiona Smith, Susanna Forbes, Deirdre Headon, Gaelle Lochner, Jamie Ambrose, Hannah McEwen and the entire Mitchell Beazley crew for yet another painless ride! Also, big thanks to Hardie Grant and Cosmos for publishing The Juice around the globe. Barry, Tony and the team at Prospect Pictures (Saturday Cooks, Great Food Live, Taste & Food Uncut)

Oz Clarke, Robert Joseph, Anthony Rose, Max Allen, David Gleave MW, Jancis Robinson MW, Neal Martin, Philip Rich, Bob Campbell MW and James Halliday – for support, good advice and/or constructive words of encouragement at some stage over the past year. Thank you.

My amazing Mum (xox), Drew, Caroline, Jesse, Eve, Anne, Thommo, Gin, Camilla and Felix, Team Grind; Tobe, Randy and Scotty, Gyros, BP and CC, Jamie and Jools, Jimmy and Caela, Simon and Hayley, Bobs and Tommy, Pete and Dolly, Danny McCubbin, Donald Stuart Gregor III and Cam Mackenzie, Andy Frost, The Jones and Duncan clans, Andy Carlton (for the killer tunes), Charles Back, Frank and John Van, Danny Colls (god, I miss your coffee mate), The River Café team, Victoria Bitter, You Am I, The Hawks, and beautiful Melbourne town – love and miss you all.
M x